CROCHET

CAVENDISH HOUSE

CROCHET

Contents

Crochet Abbreviation

alt	alternate(ly)
approx	approximate(ly)
beg	begin(ning)
ch	chain
cont	continu(e)(ing)
dec	decrease
dc	double crochet
dtr	double treble
foll	follow(ing)
gr(s)	group(s)
htr	half treble
in	inch(es)
inc	increase
No.	Number
patt	pattern
rem	remain(ing)
rep	repeat
RS	right side
ss	slip stitch
sp	space
st(s)	stiches(es)
tog	together
tr	treble
tr tr	triple treble
WS	wrong side
yd(s)	Yard(s)
Yrh	yarn round hook

Hook Sizes

ISR	US
0.60	14 Boye
0.75	12 Boye
1.00	10 Boye
1.50	7 Boye
1.75	4 Boye
2.00	1 Boye or B Bernat
2.50	0 Boye or D Bernat
3.00	F Bernat
3.50	G Bernat
4.00	H Bernat
4.50	I Bernat
5.00	J Bernat
5.50	I Boye
6.00	J Boye
7.00	K Boye

Pictures supplied by

Beta 30. Tony Boases 42. Stuart Brown 19. John Carter 8, 9, 15. Roger Charity 3, 4, 25-27. Richard Dunkley 4, 5. Geoffrey Frosch 56/57. Tony Horth 22/3. Jeany 18, 44/5. Peter Kibbles 63. Chris Lewis 37, 43, 48, 49, 60, 61. Sandra Lousada 16/17. Jean Paul Froget 55. Peter Pugh Cook 12, 20, 31, 24, 29, 35, 40, 46, 50/1. Simis 39. John Swannell 13. Rupert Watts 1, 33, 52/3, 64.

Spinners' addresses

Coats J & P Coats Limited, Central Office, 12 Seedhill Road, Paisley, Scotland.
Lee Target – George Lee & Sons, P.O. Box 37, Providence Mills, Wakefield, Yorks.
Lister – Lister & Co., P.O. Box 37, Providence Mills, Wakefield, Yorks.
Patons – Jaeger Hand Knitting Limited, McMullen Road, Darlington, Co. Durham.
Pingouin – French Wools Limited, 7-11 Lexington Street, London W1R 4BU.
Robin – Robin Wools Limited, Robin Mills, Idle, Bradford BD10 9TE.
Sirdar – Sirdar Limited, P.O. Box 31, Bective Mills, Alverthorpe, Wakefield, Yorks.
3 Suisses – Filiature de l'Espierres, 13 Saffron Way, Leicester.
Twilleys – H.G. Twilley Limited, Roman Mills, Stamford, Lincs. PE9 1BG.
Wendy – Carter & Parker Limited, Gordon Mills, Netherfield Road, Guisely, Yorks. LS20 9PD.

Editor   Pam Dawson
Assitant Editor   Heather Marco

Published by
Marshall Cavendish Limited
58 Old Compton Street
London WV1 5PA

© Marshall Cavendish Limited 1974 82

ISBN 0 85685 273 2
Printed in Yugoslavia

CROCHET

Crochet is one of the most popular and versatile of all the needlecrafts. It can be used to make warm durable garments and accessories and fine, delicate baby clothes as well as elegant evening garments. The range of yarns available is every bit as extensive and colourful as that for knitting.

This collection of beautifully illustrated designs has something for everyone. For ladies there are chic winter coats, cardigans and evening tops as well as hats, bags and accessories. For babies, a traditional shawl and bonnet, a bright cape, sun-suit and matching dress and hat, plus many more. For your home we include in this truly comprehensive collection cushions, table mats, curtains and bedcovers – even a shaggy bear bath mat. So start today and make these lovely items for yourself, your family and your home

Classic crochet coat

Sizes
To fit 81.5 [86.5:91.5:96.5] cm (*32 [34:36: 38] in*) bust
Length to shoulder, 106.5 [106.5:109:109] cm (*42[42:43:43] in*)
Sleeve seam, 42 [42:44.5:44.5] cm (*16½ [16½:17½:17½] in*) excluding cuff
The figures in brackets [] refer to the 86.5 (*34*), 91.5 (*36*) and 96.5cm (*38in*) sizes respectively

Tension
12 htr and 8 rows to 19cm (*3.9in*) worked on No.6.00 (ISR) crochet hook

Materials
27 [28:30:31] × 25grm balls Lister Tahiti or Lee Target Mohair
One No.5.00 (ISR) crochet book
One No.6.00 (ISR) crochet hook

Back
Using No.6.00 (ISR) hook make 72 [75: 78:81] ch.
1st row Into 3rd ch from hook work 1htr, 1htr into each ch to end. Turn. 71 [74:77:80] sts.
2nd row 2ch to count as first htr, 1htr into each htr to end, working last htr into 2nd of 2ch. Turn.
The 2nd row forms the patt.
Rep it twice more.
Next row 2ch to count as first htr, (yrh, insert hook into next st and draw through a loop) twice, yrh and draw through all 5 loops on hook – 1htr decreased –, patt to last 3htr, dec 1htr, 1htr into 2nd of 2ch. Turn.
Cont in patt, dec 1htr at each end of every foll 4th row until 53 [56:59:62] sts rem, then at each end of every foll alt row until 39 [42:45:48] sts rem. Cont without shaping until work measures 71cm (*28in*) from beg.
Next row (RS) 2ch to count as first htr, 1htr into st at base of ch, patt to last st, 2htr into 2nd of 2ch. Turn. 2 sts increased.
Cont in patt, inc one st at each end of every foll alt row until there are 49 [52:55:58] sts. Cont without shaping until work measures 89cm (*35in*) from beg, ending with a WS row.
Shape armholes
Next row Ss over first 6 [7:8:9] sts, patt to

count as first htr, patt to last 6 [7:8:9] sts, turn. 37 [38:39:40] sts.
Cont without shaping until armholes measure 18 [18:20.5:20.5] cm (*7[7:7½:7½] in*) from beg, ending with a WS row.
Shape shoulders
Next row Ss over first 5 sts, 2ch to count as first htr, patt to last 5 sts, turn.
Rep last row once more. 17 [18:19:20] sts. Fasten off.

Left front
Using No.6.00 (ISR) hook make 33 [35:36: 38] ch.
1st row Into 3rd ch from hook work 1htr, 1htr into each ch to end. Turn. 32 [34:35:37] sts.
Patt 3 rows. Cont in patt, dec one st at beg (side edge) of next and every foll 4th row until 23 [25:26:28] sts rem, then at beg of every foll alt row until 16 [18:19:21] sts rem. Cont without shaping until work measures 71cm (*28in*) from beg, ending at side edge.
Shape front and side edge
Next row 2ch to count as first htr, 1htr into st at base of ch, patt to last 3 sts, dec 1htr, 1htr into 2nd of 2ch. Turn.
Next row Patt to end. Turn.
Next row 2ch to count as first htr, 1htr into st at base of ch, patt to end. Turn.
Next row Patt to end. Turn.
Rep last 4 rows once more, then 1st and 2nd rows again. 18[20:21:23] sts. Keeping side edge straight, cont to dec at front edge as before until front measures same as back to underarm, ending at side edge.
Shape armhole
Next row Ss over first 6 [7:8:9] sts, patt to end. Turn.
Keeping armhole edge straight, cont dec at front edge as before until 10 sts rem. Cont without shaping until front matches back to shoulder, ending at armhole edge.
Shape shoulder
Next row Ss over first 5 sts, patt to end. Fasten off.

Right front
Work as given for left front, reversing shaping by dec at end instead of beg of row until work measures 71cm (*28in*) from beg, ending at front edge.

Shape front and side edge
Next row 2ch to count as first htr, dec 1htr, patt to last st, 2htr into 2nd of 2ch. Turn.
Next row Patt to end. Turn.
Next row Patt to last st, 2htr into 2nd of 2ch. Turn.
Next row Patt to end. Turn.
Complete to match left front, reversing all shapings.

Sleeves
Using No.5.00 (ISR) hook make 27 [27:29: 29] ch.
1st row Into 3rd ch from hook work 1htr, 1htr into each ch to end. Turn. 26 [26:28:28] sts.
Patt 5 rows. Change to No.6.00 (ISR) hook. Cont in patt, inc 1htr at each end of next and every foll 4th row until there are 38 [38:42:42] sts. Cont without shaping until sleeve measures 42 [42:44.5:44.5] cm (*16½ [16½:17½:17½] in*) from beg.
Shape top
Next row 2ch to count as first htr, 1htr into st at base of ch, 2htr into next st, patt to last 2 sts, 2htr into next st, 2htr into 2nd of 2ch. Turn. 42 [42:46:46] sts.
Patt 5 [5:6.5:6.5]cm (*2 [2:2½:2½] in*) more on these sts. Fasten off.

Cuffs
Using No.5.00 (ISR) hook make 16ch.
1st row Into 3rd ch from hook work 1dc, 1dc into each ch to end. Turn. 15 sts.
2nd row 1ch to count as first dc, 1dc into front loop only of each st to end. Turn.
3rd row 1ch to count as first dc, 1dc into back loop only of each st to end. Turn.
Rep last 2 rows 10 [10:11:11] times more, do not break off yarn, but.work 1 row of dc along one side of row edges. Fasten off.

Belt
Using No.5.00 (ISR) hook make 151ch.
Work first 3 rows as given for cuff. Rep 2nd and 3rd rows twice more. Fasten off.

To make up
Press each piece under a dry cloth with a cool iron. Join shoulder seams. Set in sleeves, sewing row ends of top shaping to sts left at underarms. Join side and sleeve seams. Join short edges of cuffs. Join cuff to sleeve by placing RS of untrimmed edge of cuff to RS of sleeve and working through the 2 thicknesses in dc.
Front edging Using No.5.00 (ISR) hook and with RS of work facing, work a row of dc all round front edge (working approx 3dc into every 2 row ends). Rep 2nd and 3rd rows as given for cuffs 3 times more. Fasten off.
Make a belt loop at either side of waist. Press seams.

Clutch purse and bandeau

Sizes
Bandeau to fit an average size head
Clutch purse measures 25.5cm (*10in*) wide × 12.5cm (*5in*) deep

Tension
22 sts and 20 rows to 10cm (*3.9in*) over htr worked with a No.3.50 (ISR) crochet hook

Materials
3 × 25gm balls Twilley's Crysette in main shade, A
1 ball of contrast colour, B
1 ball of contrast colour, C
2 pieces of lining fabric, 25.5cm (*10in*) deep × 28cm (*11in*) wide
2 pieces of card, 12.5cm (*5in*) × 25.5cm (*10in*), optional.

Bandeau
Using No.3.50 (ISR) hook and A, make 118ch. Join with a ss into first ch to form a circle.
1st round 2ch to count as first htr, miss first ch, one htr into each ch to end. Join with a ss into 2nd of 2ch. 118htr.
2nd round Working 2ch to count as first htr on every round, miss first st, one htr into every st to end. Join with a ss into 2nd of 2ch.
Rep 2nd round twice more. Join in B and work 2 rounds. Join in C and work one round, then work 2 rounds more with B. Break off B and C. Cont with A for 4 rounds.
Next round 1ch to count as first dc, miss first st, 1dc into every st to end. Join with a ss to first ch. Fasten off.

Loop
Using No.3.50 (ISR) hook and A, make 22ch. Join with a ss into first ch so enclosing bandeau
1st round 2ch to count as first htr, miss first ch, one htr into each ch to end. Join with a ss into 2nd of 2ch. 22htr.
2nd round Working 2ch to count as first htr on every round, miss first st, one htr into each st to end. Join with a ss into 2nd of 2ch.
Rep 2nd round twice more. Fasten off.

Clutch purse
Using No.3.50 (ISR) hook and A, make 110ch. Join with a ss to first ch to form a circle.
1st round 2ch to count as first htr, miss first ch, 1htr into each ch to end. Join with a ss into 2nd of 2ch. 110htr.
2nd round Working 2ch to count as first htr on every round, miss first st, 1htr into every st to end. Join with a ss into 2nd of 2ch.
Rep 2nd round until work measures 15cm (*6in*) from beg. Fasten off but do not break yarn.

Purse bandeau
Using No.3.50 (ISR) hook and A, make 64ch. Join with a ss into first ch to form a circle. Work as given for bandeau.

Loop
Work as for bandeau loop but enclosing purse bandeau.

To make up
Darn in all ends. Press under a damp cloth with a warm iron.
Clutch purse Turn work and yarn through to WS. Hold bag tog to make a back and front, with the ss at the side seam. To seam the lower edge, work 1ch to count as first dc, miss first st and work 1dc into each pair of sts to end. Fasten off. Press. Using the lining double, fold in half lengthways, RS tog, and join the side seams taking 1.5cm (*½in*) turnings. If required insert the card between the two layers of lining. Place lining in position in purse. Turn down 2.5cm (*1in*) at top edge of purse and sl st to lining. Press.

Casual waistcoat

Sizes
To fit 81.5[86.5:91.5]cm (32[34:36]in) bust
Length to shoulder, 58.5[59.5:61]cm (23[23½:24]in)
The figures in brackets [ ] refer to the 86.5 (34) and 91.5cm (36in) sizes respectively.

Tension
18 sts and 10 rows to 10cm (3.9in) over tr worked on No.3.50 (ISR) crochet hook

Materials
4[4:5] × 50grm balls Patons Kismet in main random dyed shade, A
1[1:1] ball of contrast colour, B
One No.3.00 (ISR) crochet hook
One No.3.50 (ISR) crochet hook
One No.4.00 (ISR) crochet hook

Back
Using No.4.00 (ISR) hook and A, make 78 [82:86]ch.
1st row Into 4th ch from hook work 1tr, work 1tr into each ch to end. Turn. 76 [80:84] sts.
Change to No.3.50 (ISR) hook. Cont in tr for 38cm (15in).
Shape armholes
Next row Ss over first 6 sts, patt to last 6 sts, turn.
Next row 3ch, dec one st, patt to last 3 sts, dec one st, 1tr into 3rd of 3ch. Turn.
Rep last row until 54[56:58]sts rem. Cont without shaping until armholes measure 17.5[19:20.5]cm (7[7½:8]in) from beg.
Shape shoulders
Next row Ss over first 4 sts, 1dc into each of next 4 sts, 1htr into each of next 4 sts, 1tr into each of next 5 sts, fasten off, miss next 20 [22:24] sts, rejoin yarn to next st, 3ch, 1tr into each of next 4 sts, 1 htr into each of next 4 sts, 1dc into each of next 4 sts. Fasten off.

Left front
Using No.4.00 (ISR) hook and A, make 36 [38:40]ch.
1st row Into 4th ch from hook work 1tr, work 1tr into each ch to end. Turn. 34[36:40] sts.
Change to No.3.50 (ISR) hook. Cont in tr until 6 rows less than back to armhole have been worked.
Shape front edge
Next row Patt to last 3 sts, dec one st, 1tr into 3rd of 3ch. Turn.

Patt 2 rows without shaping.
Next row 3ch, dec one st, patt to end. Turn. Patt 2 rows without shaping.
Shape armhole
Next row Ss over first 6 sts, patt to last 3 sts, dec one st, 1tr into 3rd of 3ch. Turn.
Cont to dec one st at front edge on every foll 3rd row, *at the same time* dec one st at armhole edge, inside one st border as before on every row until 19[19:20] sts rem. Keeping armhole edge straight, cont to dec at front edge only until 17 sts rem. Cont without shaping until armhole measures same as back to shoulder, ending at armhole edge.
Shape shoulder
Next row Ss over first 4 sts, 1dc into each of next 4 sts, 1htr into each of next 4 sts, 1tr into each of next 5 sts. Fasten off.

Right front
Work as given for left front.

Pocket
Using No.4.00 (ISR) hook and A, make 23ch.
1st row Into 4th ch from hook work 1tr, work 1tr into every ch to end. Turn. 21sts.
Change to No.3.50 (ISR) hook. Work 9 more rows in tr. Fasten off A. Change to No.3.00 (ISR) hook. Join in B and work 5 rows in dc for border. Fasten off.

To make up
Join shoulder and side seams. Sew pocket in position.
Edging Using No.3.00 (ISR) hook, B and with RS of work facing, work in dc all round outer edge (working 2dc into every row end along front edges, 3dc into corner sp at lower edge of each front and 1dc into each st along lower edge and back neck). Work 5 more rounds in dc, inc at each corner on every round. Fasten off.
Work similar edging round armholes.

Soft silky sweater for day or evening wear

Sizes

To fit 81.5 [86.5:91.5:96.5:101.5:106.5] cm (*32[34:36:38:40:42]in*) bust.
Length to shoulder, 66[66:67.5:67.5:68.5: 68.5) cm (*26[26:26½:26½:27:27]in*)
Sleeve seam, 35.5cm (*14in*)
The figures in brackets [] refer to the 86.5 86.5 (*34*), 91.5 (*36*), 101.5 (*38*) and 106.5cm (*42in*) sizes respectively

Tension

4 patt repeats and 12 rows to 7.5cm (*3in*) over patt worked on No.2.50 (ISR) crochet hook

Materials

9 [9:10:10:11:11] × 20grm balls Twilley's Lystwist in main shade, A
9 [9:10:10:11:11] balls each of contrast colours, B and C
One No.2.50 (ISR) crochet hook

Back yoke

Using No.2.50 (ISR) hook and A, make 128 [134:146:152:164:170] ch.
Base row Into 2nd ch from hook work 1dc, *1ch, miss next ch, 1dc into next ch, 2ch, miss next ch, 1dc into next ch, 1ch, miss 1ch, 1dc into next ch, rep from * to end. Turn. Commence patt.
1st row (RS) Using A, 1ch, 1dc into st at base of ch, *miss 1ch and 1dc, 5tr into next 2ch sp, miss next dc and ch, 1dc into next dc, rep from * to end. Turn. 21 [22:24:25:27:28] patt repeats.
2nd row Using B, 1ch, 1dc into st at base of ch, *1ch, 1dc into 2nd tr of 5tr gr, 2ch, 1dc into 4th tr of 5th gr, 1ch, 1dc into next dc, rep from * to end.
Turn.
3rd row Using B, as 1st row.

4th row Using C, as 2nd row.
5th row Using C, as 1st row.
6th row Using A, as 2nd row.
These 6 rows form patt and are rep throughout.

Shape armholes

1st row Ss over first 4dc, 1ch, patt to end. Turn. 1 patt repeat dec.
2nd row Ss over first dc, 5tr gr and into next dc, 1ch, patt to end. Turn. 1 patt repeat dec.
Rep last 2 rows once more. 17 [18:20:21:23: 24] patt reps. **. Cont without shaping until work measures 19 [19:20.5:20.5:21.5: 21.5]cm (*7½ [7½:8:8:8½:8½] in*) from beg, ending with a RS row.

Shape neck

Next row Patt across first 5 [5:6:6:7:7] patt repeats, turn.
Complete this side first. Work 1 row.
Next row Patt across first 4[4:5:5:6:6] patt reps, turn.
Work 1 row. Fasten off.
With WS of work facing, return to beg of neck shaping. Leave next 7[8:8:9:9:10] patt repeats for centre back neck, rejoin yarn to next st and patt to end. Complete to match first side, reversing shaping.

Front yoke

Work as given for back yoke to **.
Cont without shaping until work measures 11.5[11.5:12.5:12.5:14:14]cm (*4½ [4½:5:5: 5½:5½]in*) from beg, ending with a RS row.

Shape neck

Next row Patt across first 6[6:7:7:8:8] patt repeats, turn.
Complete this side first. Work 1 row.
Next row Patt to last patt repeat, turn.
1 patt repeat dec.
Work 1 row. Rep last 2 rows once more.

4[4:5:5:6:6] patt repeats. Cont without shaping until work matches back to shoulder. Fasten off.

With WS of work facing, return to beg of neck shaping, leave next 5[6:6:7:7:8] patt repeats for centre front neck, rejoin yarn to next st and patt to end. Complete to match first side, reversing shaping.

Back main part
Using No. 2.50 (ISR) hook, C and with RS of back yoke facing, beg at right-hand edge of commencement ch and work across yoke as foll:

1ch, 1dc into first dc, *5tr into next ch sp opposite 5tr gr on yoke, 1dc into dc between 5tr grs, rep from * to end.

Cont in patt as given for back yoke, working in stripe sequence of 2 rows B, 2 rows A and 2 rows C, until work measures 66[66:67.5: 67.5:68.5:68.5]cm (*26[26:26½:26½:27:27]in*) from shoulder, ending with a 1st patt row. Fasten off.

Front main part
Work as given for back.

Sleeves
Using No. 2.50 (ISR) hook and A, make 32[32:38:38:44:44] ch and beg at top. Work base row as given for back yoke.
5[5:6:6:7:7] patt repeats.

Shape top
1st row Using A, 1ch, 1dc into st at base of ch, *miss 1dc, 5tr into next 2ch sp, miss 1dc, 1dc into next dc, rep from * to end, make 7ch, turn.

2nd row Using C, 1dc into 2nd ch from hook, 1ch, miss 1ch, 1dc into next ch, 2ch, miss 1ch, 1dc into next ch, 1ch, miss 1ch, 1dc into next dc, *1ch, 1dc into 2nd of 5tr gr, 2ch, 1dc into 4th tr of 5tr gr, 1ch, 1dc into next dc, rep from * to end, make 7ch, turn. 1 patt rep inc.

3rd row Using C, 1dc into 2nd ch from hook, miss 2ch, 5tr into next ch, miss 2ch, 1dc into next dc, *miss 1dc, 5tr into next 2ch sp, miss 1dc, 1dc into next dc, rep from * to end, make 7ch, turn.

Cont working in stripe sequence of 2 rows B, 2 rows A and 2 rows C, *at the same time* inc 1 patt repeat in this way until 6 patts have been inc at each side. 17[17:18:18:19:19] patt repeats. Cont in patt without shaping for a further 35.5cm (*14in*). Fasten off.

Neckband
Join shoulder seams. Using No.2.50 (ISR) hook, C and with RS of work facing, beg at left shoulder seam and work 2 rounds dc around neck edge. Fasten off.

To make up
Set in sleeves. Join side and sleeve seams. Press seams lightly.

Colourful winter lounger

Sizes
To fit 81.5 [86.5:91.5:96.5:101.5] cm
(32 [34:36:38:40] in) bust
This wrap can be made in two lengths:
Long wrap length to shoulder, 134.5
[134.5:136:136:136] cm (53 [53:53½:53½:
53½] in)
Short wrap length to shoulder, 101.5
[101.5:103:103:103] cm (40 [40:40½:40½:
40½] in)
Sleeve seam, 47cm (18½in)
The figures in brackets [] refer to the 86.5
(34), 91.5 (36), 96.5 (38) and 101.5cm (40in)
sizes respectively

Tension
2tr grs to 4.5cm (1¾in) measured from
centre of each gr and 12 rows to 10cm
(3.9in) worked on No.3.50 (ISR) hook

Materials
Long wrap 7 [8:8:8:8] × 50grm balls
Coton du Pingouin No. 5 in main shade, A
5 [6:6:6:6] balls of contrast colour, B
6 [6:6:7:7] balls of contrast colour, C
4 [5:5:5:5] balls of contrast colour , D
2 [2:3:3:3] balls of contrast colour, E
Short wrap 7 [8:8:8:8] balls of same in
main shade, A
4 [5:5:5:5] balls of contrast colour, B
4 [4:4:4:4] balls of contrast colour, C
4 [4:5:5:5] balls of contrast colour, D
2[2:2:2:3] balls of contrast colour, E
One No.3.50 (ISR) crochet hook
7 buttons for long wrap
6 buttons for short wrap

Long wrap back
(worked from shoulder)
Using No.3.50 (ISR) hook and D, make
74 [79:84:94:99] ch.
1st row Into 6th ch from hook work 5tr,
*1ch, miss 4ch, 5tr into next ch, rep from *
to last 3ch, 1tr into last ch. Turn. 14
[15:16:18:19] tr gr.
2nd row 3ch to count as first tr, 2tr into
same st as 3ch, *1ch, 5tr into next 1ch sp,
rep from * to last 5tr gr, 1ch, 3tr into last st.
Turn. (½ patt at each end of row.)
3rd row 3ch, 5tr into next 1ch sp, *1ch, 5tr
into next 1ch sp, rep from * to end, 1tr into
last st. Turn.

The 2nd and 3rd rows from patt. Rep 2nd
row once more. Break off D and join in B.
Beg with 3rd row work 14 [14:16:16:16]
rows in patt, ending with a 2nd row.
Shape armholes
Next row 3ch to count as first tr, 2tr into
same st as 3ch, 1ch, 5tr into next 1ch sp, patt
to last 1ch sp, 5tr into last 1ch sp, 1ch, 3tr into
last st. Turn.
Rep last row 4 times more. 19 [20:21:23:24]
tr grs. (½ patt at each end to count as 1 patt.)
Fasten off.

Left front
(worked from shoulder)
Using No.3.50 (ISR) hook and D, make
24 [24:29:29:34] ch. Work first row as
given for back. 4 [4:5:5:6] tr grs. Cont in
patt as given for back, work 5 rows. Break
off D and join in B. Work 8 [8:10:10:10]
more rows in patt. **.
Shape neck
1st row 3ch to count as first tr, 2tr into
same st as 3ch, 1ch, 5tr into next 1ch sp, patt
to end. Turn.
2nd row Patt to last 1ch sp, 5tr into last
1ch sp, 1ch, 3tr into last st. Turn.
Rep last 2 rows twice more, working 7ch

at end of last row.
Next row Into 6th ch from hook work 5tr,
1ch, miss next ch and 3tr, 5tr into next 1ch
sp, pattt to last 1ch sp, 5tr into last 1ch sp,
1ch, 3tr into last st. Turn.
Shape armhole
Keeping neck edge straight, rep first and
2nd neck shaping rows twice to shape
armhole. 10½ [10½:11½:11½:12½] tr grs.
Fasten off.

Right front
Work as given for left front to **
Shape neck
1st row Work in patt to last 1ch sp, 5tr into
this sp, 1ch, 3tr into last st. Turn.
2nd row 3ch to count as first tr, 2tr into
same st as 3ch, 1ch, 5tr into next 1ch sp,
patt to end. Turn.
Rep these 2 rows twice more.
Next row 3ch to count as first tr, 2tr into
same st, 1ch, 5tr into next sp, patt until one
½ patt rem, ending with 5tr into last sp,
using another ball of yarn, ss into end of
previous row at neck edge, work 7ch and
fasten off, return to working st at end of
last row, 1ch, miss ½ patt and first 5ch just
worked, 5tr into next ch, 1tr into last ch.
Turn.
Shape armhole
Keeping neck edge straight, rep first and 2nd
neck shaping rows twice to shape armhole.
10½ [10½:11½:11½:12½] tr grs. Fasten off.

Skirt
(worked downwards from armholes)
With RS of work facing, rejoin B to lower
edge of left front, patt across all pieces as foll:
Next row Patt across left front until ½ patt
rem, ending with 5tr into last 1ch sp and
mark this sp with coloured thread, 5tr into

first 1ch sp of back, patt across back, ending with 5tr into last 1ch sp, 1ch and mark this ch with coloured thread, 5tr into first 1ch sp of right front at armhole edge, patt to end. Turn. 40 [41:44:46:49] tr grs. (½ patt at each end counts as 1 patt.) Break off B and join in E. Work throughout in stripes of 4 rows E, 19 rows A, 13 rows C, 11 rows D, 9 rows B, 6 rows E, 26 rows A, 21 rows C, 9 rows D, 3 rows E and 9 rows B, *at the same time* shape sides as foll:

Next row Patt across right front to coloured marker, (5tr, 1ch) twice into 1ch sp, work across back to coloured marker, (5tr, 1ch) twice into 1ch sp, patt to end, Turn. 1tr gr has been increased below each armhole.

Patt 6 rows without shaping. Rep last 7 rows 17 times more, working inc above those in previous row. 76 [77:80:82:85] tr grs. Cont without shaping until 9th row of last B stripe has been completed. Fasten off.

Sleeves

(worked from top)
Using No.3.50 (ISR) hook and D, make 24ch. Work first row as given for back. 4 tr grs.

2nd row As 2nd row of back.

3rd row 3ch to count as first tr, 2tr into same st, 1ch, patt to end, working 5tr into last 1ch sp, 3tr into last st. Turn.

4th row As 3rd row of back.
Rep 2nd–4th rows once more. Break off D and join in B. Rep 2nd and 3rd rows once more, then work 3rd row 7 [7:8:8:8] times more.

Next row As 2nd row. 14 [14:15:15:15] tr grs.

Break off D and join in E. Cont without shaping, working 23 rows in stripe sequence of 4 rows E and 19 rows A, ending with a 2nd patt row. Break off A and join in C. Working in stripes of 13 rows C, 11 rows D and 9 rows B, *at the same time* shape sides as foll:

Next row 3ch to count as first tr, 2tr into same st as 3ch, 5tr into first 1ch sp, patt to last 1ch sp, 5tr into this ch sp, 1ch, 3tr into last st. Turn. ½ patt has been increased at each end.

Patt 6 rows without shaping. Rep last 7 rows 3 times more. 18 [18:19:19:19] tr grs. Cont without shaping until 9th row of B stripe has been worked. Fasten off.

To make up

Press under a damp cloth with a warm iron. Join shoulder seams, noting that first row of fronts from shoulder shaping for back. **Edging** Using No.3.50 (ISR) hook, B and with RS of work facing, work 1 row dc up right front edge, round neck and down left

front edge. Mark positions for 7 buttons on left front, first come to at neck, and last 43cm (*17in*) from lower edge with the others evenly spaced between.

Next row 1dc into each dc of previous row, working 3dc into corners at neck and making buttonholes as markers are reached by missing 2dc and working 7ch over these 2dc.

Next row 1dc into each dc of previous row, working 3dc into corners and 8dc into each buttonhole. Fasten off.
Join sleeve seams. Set in sleeves. Sew on

buttons to correspond with buttonholes. Press seams and borders.

Short wrap

As given for long wrap, working inc rows 11 times only on skirt and ending after 26 rows in A have been worked.

To make up

Press as given for long wrap. Complete as given for long wrap, working 6 buttonholes only.

Size
To fit an average head

Tension
12htr and 9 rows to 5cm (*2in*) over patt worked on No.3.50 (ISR) crochet hook

Materials
1 × 25grm ball Lee Target Motoravia 4 ply in each of 5 colours, A, B, C, D and E
One No.3.50 (ISR) crochet hook

Note
When using two different coloured yarns in the same round, always work over the colour not in use and when changing colour, draw the new colour through all the loops on the hook of the last st in the old colour.

Hat
Using No.3.50 (ISR) hook and A, make 6ch. Join with a ss into first ch to form circle.
1st round Using A, 2ch to count as first htr, 7htr into circle. Join with a ss into 2nd of 2ch. 8htr.
Break off A.
2nd round Using B, 2ch, 1htr into st at base of ch, *2htr into next htr, rep from * to end. Join with a ss into 2nd of 2ch. 16htr.
3rd round Using 4 sts each of B and C all round, work 2ch, 2htr into next htr, *1htr into next htr, 2 htr into next htr, rep from * to end.
Join with a ss into 2nd of 2ch. 24htr.
Break off B and C.
4th round Using D, 2ch, 1htr into next htr, 2htr into next htr, *1htr into each of next 2htr, 2htr into next htr, rep from * to end. Join with a ss into 2nd of 2ch. 32htr.
5th round Using 5 sts each of D and E all round, work 2ch, 1htr into each of next 2htr, 2htr into next htr, *1htr into each of next 3htr, 2htr into next htr, rep from * to end. Join with a ss into 2nd of 2ch. 40 htr. Break off E.
6th round Using D, 2ch, 1htr into each of next 3htr, 2htr into next htr, *1htr into each of next 4htr, 2htr into next htr, rep from * to end. Join with a ss into 2nd of 2ch. 48htr. Break off D.
7th round Using C, 2ch, 1htr into each of next 4htr, 2htr into next htr, *1htr into each of next 5htr, 2htr into next htr, rep from * to end. Join with a ss into 2nd of 2ch. 56htr. Break off C.
8th round Using A, 2ch, 1htr into each of next 5htr, 2htr into next htr, *1htr into each of next 6htr, 2htr into next htr, rep from * to end. Join with a ss into 2nd of 2ch. 64htr.
9th round Using A, 2ch, 1htr into each of next 6htr, 2htr into next htr, *1htr into each of next 7htr, 2htr into next htr, rep from * to end. Join with a ss into 2nd of 2ch. 72htr.
Break off A.

olour cloche hat

10th round Using E, 2ch, 1htr into each of next 7htr, 2htr into next htr, *1htr into each of next 8htr, 2htr into next htr, rep from * to end. Join with a ss into 2nd of 2ch. 80htr. Break off E.

11th round Using 4 sts each of B and D all round, 2ch, 1htr into each of next 8htr, 2htr into next htr, * 1htr into each of next 9htr, 2htr into next htr, rep from * to end. Join with a ss into 2nd of 2ch. 88htr.

12th round Using 4 sts each of B and D and working into same colours in previous round, 2ch, 1htr into each htr to end. Join with a ss into 2nd of 2ch. Break off B and D.

13th round Using E, as 12th. Break off E.

14th round Using C, as 12th. Break off C.

15th round Using B, as 12th. Break off B.

16th round Using one st of A and 7 sts of D all round, as 12th.

17th round Using 3 sts of A and 5 sts of D all round, as 12th. Break off A and D.

18th round Using E, as 12th. Break off E.

19th round Using A, as 12th.

20th round Using 4 sts of A and 4 sts of C all round, as 12th.

21st round As 20th. Break off A and C.

22nd round Using B, as 12th. Break off B.

23rd round Using A, as 12th.

24th round Using C, as 12th.

25th round Using 3 sts of B and 5 sts of E all round, as 12th. Break off B and E.

26th round Using D, as 12th.

27th round As 26th.

Shape brim

28th round Using E, 2ch, 2htr into next htr, *1htr into next htr, 2htr into next htr, rep from * to end. Join with a ss into 2nd of 2ch. 132htr. Break off E.

29th round Using B, as 12th. Break off B.

30th round Using C, as 12th. Break off C.

31st round Using 8 sts of A and 4 sts of E all round, as 12th. Break off A and E.

32nd round Using D, 2ch, 1htr into each of next 4htr, 2htr into next htr, *1htr into each of next 5htr, 2htr into next htr, rep from * to end. Join with a ss into 2nd of 2ch. 154htr. Break off D.

33rd round Using A, as 12th.

34th round Using 4 sts of A and 3 sts of B all round, as 12th. Break off A and B.

35th round Using E, 2ch, 1htr into each of next 5htr, 2htr into next htr, *1htr into each of next 6htr, 2htr into next htr, rep from * to end. Join with a ss into 2nd of 2ch. 176htr. Break off E.

36th round Using D, as 12th. Break off D.

37th round Using C and working from left to right (i.e. in a backwards direction), work 1dc into each htr to end. Join with a ss into first dc. Fasten off.

Gay gypsy scarf

Size
106.5cm (*42in*) long from point to point and
12.5cm (*5in*) wide

Tension
4 ch loops to 11.5cm (*4½in*) and 7 rows to

7.5cm (*3in*) over patt worked on No.5.00
(ISR) crochet hook

Materials
1 × 50grm ball Sirdar Sportswool
One No.5.00 (ISR) crochet hook

Scarf
Using No.5.00 (ISR) hook work 143ch.
Base row Into 3rd ch from hook work 1dc,
*5ch, miss 3ch, 1dc into next ch, rep from *
to end. Turn. 35 ch loops.
Commence patt.
1st row Ss to centre ch of first loop, 1dc
into centre ch, *5ch, 1dc into centre ch of
next 5ch loop, rep from * to end. Turn.
Rep last row 8 times more.
Next row Ss to centre ch of first loop, 1dc
into centre ch, *3ch, 1dc into centre ch of
next 5ch loop, rep from * to end. Fasten off.

To make up
Press lightly under a damp cloth with a
warm iron.

Three colour winter scarf

Size
23cm (*9in*) wide × 203.5cm (*84in*) long, excluding fringe

Tension
4 sp and approx 6 rows to 10cm (*3.9in*) over patt worked on No.5.50 (ISR) crochet hook

Materials
3 × 50grm balls Grosvenor Double Knitting by 3 Suisses in main shade, A
2 balls of contrast colour, B
1 ball of contrast colour, C
One No.5.50 (ISR) crochet hook

Note
When using C and last ball of A work from centre and outside of ball at same time

Scarf
Using No.5.50 (ISR) hook and 2 strands of A, make 35ch. Commence patt using 2 strands of yarn throughout.

Base row Into 5th ch from hook work 1dc, *5ch, miss 4ch, 1dc into next ch, rep from * to end.
Turn. 7 ch sp.

1st row 4ch, 1dc into first sp, *5ch, 1dc into next sp, rep from * to end. Turn. 7 ch sp.
The last row forms patt. Cont in patt working in stripe sequence of 18 more rows A, 10 rows B, 10 rows C, 10 rows B, 30 rows A, 10 rows B, 10 rows C, 10 rows B and 20 rows A.
Fasten off.

To make up
Darn in all ends.
Fringe Cut rem A and C into lengths approx 45.5cm (*18in*) long. Using 4 strands of A and C, knot a tassel through each ch sp on both short ends.
Trim tassels.

A simple cover-up snood

Size
To fit average head with long hair

Tension
4 ch loops and 6 rows to 10cm (*3.9in*) over patt worked on No.4.50 (ISR) hook

Materials
1 × 50grm ball Patons Double Knitting in main shade, A
Oddment of contrast colour, B
One No.4.50 (ISR) crochet hook

Snood
Using No.4.50 (ISR) hook and A, make 82ch.
Base row Into 3rd ch from hook work 1dc, 1dc into each ch to end. Turn. 81dc.
Next row 1ch to count as first dc, miss first dc, 1dc into each dc to end, working last dc into turning ch and joining in B by drawing a ch through loop on hook.
Turn.
Using B, work 2 rows dc. Break off B.
Join in A. Work one more row dc. Cont with A only.
Next row 8ch, miss first 4dc, 1dc into next dc, *7ch, miss 3dc, 1dc into next dc, rep from * to end. Turn. 20 ch loops.
Next row 7ch, 1dc into centre ch of first loop, *7ch, 1dc into centre ch of next loop, rep from * to end. Turn.
Next row *7ch, 1dc into centre ch of next ch loop, rep from * to end, working last dc into centre ch of 7 turning ch. Turn.
Rep last row 12 times more.
Next row *7ch, 1dc into centre ch of next two ch loops working the two loops tog, rep from * to end, working last ch loop and turning ch tog. Turn. 10 ch loops.
Rep last row once more. 5 ch loops.
Next row 7ch, 1dc into centre ch of each ch loop keeping loops of each st on hook, yrh and draw through all loops on hook.
Fasten off.

To make up
Press under a damp cloth with a warm iron.
Join seam.

14

A shawl using granny squares

Size
106.5cm (*42in*) square excluding fringe

Tension
Each motif measures 9cm (*3½in*) square worked on No.3.00 (ISR) crochet hook

Materials
29 × 20grm balls Wendy Tricel–Nylon Crepe 4 ply
One No.3.00 (ISR) crochet hook

First border motif
Using No.3.00 (ISR) hook make 4ch. Join with a ss to first ch to form circle.

1st round 1ch to count as first dc, 7dc into circle. Join with a ss into first ch.

2nd round 4ch to count as first dtr, 5dtr into first st, remove hook from working loop and insert into top of first dtr, reinsert hook into working loop and pull through st on hook – thus making a raised petal –, 2ch, *6dtr into next st, make a raised petal, 2ch, rep from * 6 times more. Join with a ss to top of first raised petal.

3rd round Ss into first ch sp, 3ch to count as first tr, 2tr into same sp, 2ch, *3tr into next ch sp, 2ch, rep from * 6 times more. Join with a ss into 3rd of the 3ch.

4th round 3ch to count as first tr, 1tr into first st, 1tr into next st, 2tr into next tr, 2ch, *2tr into next tr, 1tr into next st, 2tr into next tr, 2ch, rep from * 6 times more. Join with a ss into 3rd of the 3ch.

5th round 3ch to count as first tr, leaving last loop of each on hook work 1tr into each of next 4tr, yrh and draw through all loops on hook, *3ch, 1dc into next ch sp, 3ch, 1tr into each of next 5tr, 3ch, 1dc into next ch sp, 3ch, leaving last loop of each on hook work 1tr into each of next 5tr, yrh and draw through all loops on hook – 1 cluster worked –, rep from * twice more, 3ch, 1dc into next

ch sp, 3ch, 1tr into each of next 5tr, 3ch, 1dc
into next ch sp, 3ch. Join with a ss into top of
first cluster.
6th round 5ch, 1tr into next dc, 5ch, work a
cluster into next 5tr, 5ch, ss into top of
cluster – 1 picot worked –, *5ch, 1tr into
next dc, 5 ch, 1dc into top of next cluster, 5
ch, 1tr into next dc, 5ch, work a cluster and
picot into next 5tr, rep from * twice more,
5ch, 1tr into next dc, 5ch. Join with a ss into
first ch.

Second border motif
Work first 5 rounds as given for first border
motif.
6th round 5ch, 1tr into first dc, 5 ch, work a
cluster and picot into next 5tr, 5ch, 1tr into
next dc, 5ch, 1dc into top of next cluster, 5ch,
1tr into next dc, 5ch, work a cluster into
next 5tr, with WS tog place 2nd motif
against first motif, 1ch, ss into corner picot of
first motif, ss into top of cluster just
completed on 2nd motif, 2ch, ss into next
ch sp of first motif, 2ch, 1tr into next dc, 2ch,
ss into next ch sp of first motif, 2ch, 1dc into
top of next cluster, 2ch, ss into next ch sp of
first motif, 2ch, 1tr into next dc, 2ch, ss into
next ch sp of first motif, 2ch, work a cluster
into next 5tr, 1ch, ss into next corner picot of
first motif, ss into top of cluster just
completed on 2nd motif, complete as given
for first border motif.
Work and join 10 more motifs in same way
to form first row of shawl.

Second row of shawl
Work border motif and join to upper edge of
first motif in first row. Cont working
interior motifs as foll:
Using No.3.00(ISR) hook make 4ch. Join
with a ss to first ch to form circle.
1st round 1ch to count as first dc, 7dc into
circle. Join with a ss into first ch.
2nd round 5ch to count as first tr and ch sp,
*1tr into next dc, 2ch, rep from * 6 times
more. Join with a ss into 3rd of the 5ch.
3rd to 5th rounds Work as given for border
motif.
6th round Working as given for second
border motif, join to first motif of 2nd row,
then to 2nd motif of first row, then complete
round.
Work 9 more interior motifs and one border
motif to complete 2nd row of shawl. Rep
the 2nd row of shawl 9 times more, then
work and join 12 border motifs to complete
last row.

To make up
Darn in ends. Press lightly under a dry cloth.
Fringe Cut 6 ends 23cm (9in) long for each
wool, fold in half, thread folded end through
corner picot, pull cut ends through loop
thus made and knot firmly. Rep into each
ch sp and picot all round shawl.

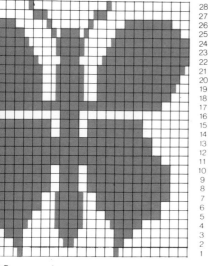

= Space and one row

= Block and one row

= Half block / half space and one row

= Beads for eyes

Sparkling top

Sizes
To fit 81.5[86.5:91.5]cm (32[34:36]in) bust
Side seam, 35.5[35.5:37]cm (14[14:14½]in)
The figures in brackets [ ] refer to the 86.5
(34) and 91.5cm (36in) sizes respectively

Tension
8 sp and 12 rows to 10cm (3.9in) over patt
worked on No.3.00 (ISR) crochet hook

Materials
3 × 20grm balls Wendy Minuit Lurex
One No.3.00 (ISR) crochet hook
3 press studs
2 glass beads for eyes

Back
Using No.3.00 (ISR) hook make 83[89:95]
ch.
Base row Into 8th ch from hook work 1tr,
*2ch, miss 2ch, 1tr into next ch, rep from *
to end. Turn.
1st row 5ch to count as first tr and 2ch, 1tr
into next tr, *2ch, 1tr into next tr, rep from *
to end, working last tr into 3rd of 7ch.
Turn. 26[28:30] sp.
Rep last row 4[4:6] times more, noting that
on subsequent rows last tr will be worked
into 3rd of 5 turning ch.
Shape sides
1st row 3ch to count as first tr, 1tr into first
tr, patt to end, working 2tr into 3rd of 5ch.
Turn.
2nd row 3ch, 1tr into first tr, 1tr into next
tr, patt to end, working 2tr into 3rd of 3ch.
Turn.
3rd row 3ch, 1tr into first tr, 1tr into each of
next 2tr, patt to last 2tr, 1tr into each of next
2tr, 2tr into 3rd of 3ch. Turn.
4th row 5ch, miss 2tr, 1tr into next tr, patt
to last 3tr, 2ch, miss 2tr, 1tr into 3rd of 3ch.
Turn. 2 sp inc.
Rep last 4 rows twice more. 32[34:36] sp.
Cont without shaping until 31[31:33] rows
in all have been worked.
Next row 3ch, *2tr into next sp, 1tr into
next tr, rep from * to end. Fasten off.

Front
Work as given for back until 2[2:4] rows
have been completed. Commence butterfly
patt.
1st row Patt 7[8:9] sp, 1ch, 1tr into next sp,
1tr into next tr, patt 10 sp, 1tr into next sp,
1ch, 1tr into next tr, patt to end. Turn.
2nd row Patt 7[8:9] sp, 1tr into next 1ch sp,
1tr into each of next 2tr (1 block of 4tr has

been worked), patt 4 sp, 1ch, 1tr into next
sp, 1tr into next tr, 1tr into next sp, 1ch, 1tr
into next tr, patt 4 sp, 1tr into next tr, 1tr
into next 1ch sp, 1tr into next tr, patt to end.
Turn.
3rd row Patt 6[7:8] sp, 2tr into next sp, 1tr
into each of next 4tr, patt 4 sp, 1tr into next
1ch sp, 1tr into each of next 3tr, 1tr into next
1ch sp, 1tr into next tr, patt 4sp, 1tr into
each of next 3tr, 2tr into sp, 1tr into next tr,
patt to end. Turn.
Cont working butterfly in this way from
chart, *at the same time* shaping sides as given
for back, until 28 rows of patt have been
completed.
Note The chart represents a filet crochet
grid of blocks, spaces, half blocks and half
spaces. Spaces are formed by working single
trebles with 2ch between them and blocks
are spaces which have been filled in by
working 2tr into the appropriate 2ch sp.
Here spaces have been subdivided into half
block/half space by working 1tr and 1ch
into a 2ch sp.
Patt one more row in sp. Work last row as
given for back.
Fasten off.

Straps (make 2)
Using No.3.00 (ISR) hook work 8ch.
1st row Into 4th ch from hook work 1tr, 1tr
into each ch to end. Turn. 6tr.
2nd row 3ch to count as first tr, 1tr into
each tr to end. Turn.
Rep 2nd row until strap measures 35.5cm
(14in) from beg, or required length. Fasten
off.

To make up
Do not press. Join right side seam. Join left
side seam to within 7.5cm (3in) of lower
edge.
Edging Using No.3.00 (ISR) hook and with
WS of work facing, rejoin yarn to first ch at
lower edge, 3ch, *2tr into first sp, 1tr into
next tr, rep from * all round lower edge.
Turn.
Next row 3ch, *1tr into next tr, rep from *
to end.
Cont working in tr up side of opening
working 1tr into each tr and 2tr into each sp,
turn and work down other side in same way.
Fasten off.
Turn edging to WS on front edge of side
opening and sl st into position to form over-
flap. Sew press studs along opening. Sew
straps in position. Sew on beads for eyes.

Mouse motif slippers

Sizes
To fit 3/4 [5/6] foot size
The figures in brackets [ ] refer to the 5/6 size only

Tension
16 sts and 18 rows to 10cm (*3.9in*) over dc worked on No.5.00 (ISR) crochet hook using 2 strands of yarn

Materials
2[3]× 40grm balls Sirdar Wash'n'Wear Double Knitting in main shade, A
Oddments of contrast colours, if required
One No.5.00 (ISR) crochet hook
One No.4.00 (ISR) crochet hook

Slippers
Using No.5.00 (ISR) hook and 2 strands of A, make 4ch. Join with a ss to first ch to form circle. Mark beg of round with coloured thread.
1st round (RS) 2ch to count as first dc, work 5dc into circle. Join with a ss to 2nd of 2ch. 6dc. Turn.
2nd round 2ch, 1dc into same place as ss, 2dc into each dc to end. Join with a ss to 2nd of 2ch. 12dc. Turn.
3rd round 2ch, 1dc into each dc to end. Join with a ss to 2nd of 2ch. Turn.
4th round 2ch, 2dc into next dc, *1 dc into next dc, 2dc into next dc, rep from * to end. Join with a ss to 2nd of 2ch. 18dc. Turn.
5th round As 3rd.
6th round 2ch, 1dc into each of next 4dc, 2dc into next dc, *1dc into each of next 5dc, 2dc into next dc, rep from * to end. Join with a ss to 2nd of 2ch. 21dc. Turn.
7th round As 3rd.
8th round 2ch, 1dc into each of next 5dc, 2dc into next dc, *1dc into each of next 6dc, 2dc into next dc, rep from * to end. Join with a ss to 2nd of 2ch. 24dc. Turn.
9th round As 3rd.
Cont inc in this way on next and every alt round 1[3] times more. 27[33]dc. Cont

without shaping, joining each round and turning, until work measures 11.5[18]cm (4½[7]*in*) from beg, ending with a WS round. Break off yarn.
Divide for instep flap and sole
Next row Using No.5.00 (ISR) hook, 2 strands of A and with RS of work facing, miss first 9[11] sts, rejoin yarn to next st, 2ch to count as first dc, 1dc into each of next 8[10]dc, turn. 9[11]dc.
Cont in dc, dec one st at each end of 5th and every row until 5 sts rem. Fasten off.
Sole
Using No.5.00 (ISR) hook, 2 strands of A and with RS of work facing, rejoin yarn to next st beyond instep flap just worked.
Next row 2ch to count as first dc, 1dc into each of next 18[22]dc, turn.
Cont in dc until work measures 24[28]cm (9½[11]*in*) from beg, or required foot length. Fasten off.
Edging
With RS facing, join centre back seam. Using No.4.00 (ISR) hook, 1 strand of A or contrast colour and with RS of work facing, beg at back seam and work 1 round dc along side, round instep flap and along other side. Join with a ss to first dc. Fasten off.

Flower motif (optional)
Using No.4.00 (ISR) hook and 1 strand of contrast colour, make 5ch. Join with a ss to first ch to form circle.
1st round 5ch to count as first dc and 3ch, (1dc, 3ch) 5 times into circle. Join with a ss to 2nd of 5ch. 6ch sp.
2nd round 1ch to count as first dc, into first 3ch sp work (1htr, 3tr, 1htr, 1dc), work (1dc, 1htr, 3tr, 1htr, 1dc) into each 3ch sp to end. Join with a ss to first ch.
3rd round *5ch, inserting hook from back of work, work 1dc round stem of dc in 1st round, rep from * 4 times more, 5ch. Join with a ss to same place as last ss.
4th round 1ch, into first 5ch sp work (1htr, 5tr, 1htr, 1dc), work (1dc, 1htr, 5tr, 1htr, 1dc) into each 5ch sp to end. Join with a ss to first ch. Fasten off.
Sew motif to centre front of slipper.

To make up
Press under a dry cloth with a cool iron. If required, make 2 small pompons in contrast colour and st to centre of commencing circle to form nose. Embroider eyes or sew on buttons. Make 2 loops for whiskers and st above nose.
Ears (make 4) Using No.4.00 (ISR) hook and 2 strands of A, make 8ch.
1st row Into 2nd ch from hook work 1dc, 1dc into each ch to end. Turn. 7dc.
Cont in dc, dec one st at each end of 5th and every row until 1dc rem. Fasten off. Sew ears in position.

A slinky sun-top

Sizes
To fit 81.5[86.5:91.5]cm (32[34:36]in) bust
The figures in brackets [ ] refer to the
86.5 (34) and 91.5cm (36in) sizes respectively

Tension
24 sts and 12 rows to 10cm (3.9in) over patt
worked on No.3.00 (ISR) crochet hook

Materials
2[2:3] × 25grm balls Sirdar Courtelle
Random
One No.3.00 (ISR) crochet hook
0.90 metres (1 yard) round elastic
4 buttons

Bandeau top

Using No.3.00 (ISR) hook make 30ch for
centre back edge.
Base row Into 4th ch from hook work 1tr,
*1ch, miss next ch, 1tr into next ch, rep from
* to end.
Turn. 13ch sp.
Commence patt.
1st row 3ch, 1tr into first tr, *1ch, 1tr into
next tr, rep from * to end.
Turn.
2nd row 3ch, 1tr into first tr, *1tr into next
ch sp, 1tr into next tr, rep from * to end.
Turn.
3rd row 3ch, 1tr into each tr to end.
Turn.
4th row 3ch, 1tr into first tr, *1ch, miss next
tr, 1tr into next tr, rep from * to end. Turn.

These 4 rows form patt. Rep them 20 [21:22]
times more, then work the 1st to 2nd rows
again.
Do not break off yarn.
Lower edging Knot one end of
elastic.
Hold elastic at lower edge of top with knot
at centre back edge, cont in dc along lower
edge, working 2 sts to each row end and
taking yarn over elastic to form casing. Cut
elastic to required length and knot, then cont
in dc up opposite side of foundation ch.
Fasten off.

To make up
Sew knots securely. Press lightly under a dry
cloth with a cool iron.
Sew 4 buttons equally spaced along last row
of top. Cut 6 strands of yarn each 305cm
(120in) long and make a twisted cord.
Knot and trim ends.
Knot cord round centre front of top, leaving
ends for ties.

Elegant halter top

Sizes
To fit 86.5/91.5cm (*34/36in*) bust

Tension
21tr and 14 rows to 10cm (*3.9in*) over patt
worked on No.2.50 (ISR) crochet hook

Materials
2 × 25grm balls Robin Tricel Nylon
Perle 4 ply in main shade, A
Oddments of 10 contrast colours
One No.2.50. (ISR) crochet hook

Top
Using No.2.50 (ISR) hook and any colour,
make 6ch. Join with a ss to first ch to form
circle.
1st row 5ch to count as first tr and 2ch sp,
3tr, 3ch, 3tr into circle, 2ch, 1tr into circle.
Break off yarn.
2nd row Join next colour to 3rd of 5ch at
beg of last row, 5ch, 3tr into first 2ch sp, 1ch,
(3tr, 3ch and 3tr) into 3ch sp, 1ch, (3tr, 2ch
and 1tr) into last 2ch sp. Break off yarn.
3rd row Join next colour to 3rd of 5ch at
beg of last row, 5ch, 3tr into first 2ch sp,
1ch, 3tr into 1ch sp, 1ch, (3tr, 3ch and 3tr)
into 3ch sp, 1ch, 3tr into 1ch sp, (3tr, 2ch and
1tr) into last 2ch sp. Break off yarn.
Cont in this way, inc one ch sp at either side
of centre and working each row in different
colour, until 28 rows in all have been
worked. Fasten off.
To make up
Darn in all ends.
Left side edging and strap Using No.2.50
(ISR) hook, A and with RS of work facing,
work 1dc into each tr up left side edge,
ending with 1dc into first ch of last 3ch sp,
make 92ch. Turn.
Next row Into 4th ch from hook work 1tr,
1tr into each ch and dc to end. Turn. 175 sts.
Next row 3ch to count as first tr, 1tr into
each tr to end. Turn.
Rep last row once more. Fasten off.
Right side edging and strap Using
No.2.50 (ISR) hook and A, make 90ch,
then with RS of work facing, work 1 dc into
first ch of 3ch at corner of triangle, 1dc into
each tr to end. Turn.
Next row 3ch, 1tr into each dc and ch to
end. Turn. 175 sts.
Next row 3ch, 1tr into each tr to end. Turn.
Rep last row once more. Fasten off.
Lower edging and straps Using No.2.50
(ISR) hook and A, make 90ch, then with RS
of work facing, work 2dc into each row end
along lower edge, then make 92ch. Turn.
Next row Into 4th ch from hook work 1tr,
1tr into each ch and dc to end. Turn. 306 sts.
Next row 3ch, 1tr into each tr to end. Fasten
off
Press work lightly under a damp cloth with
a warm iron. Stitch down cross-over at
centre front of halter strap

Evening jacket

Materials
10[11] × 20grm balls Wendy Minuit Lurex
One No.2.50 (ISR) crochet hook
One button

Sizes

To fit 81.5/91.5 [94/101.5]cm (*32/36[37/40]
in*)
Length to centre back, 40.5[43]cm
(*16[17]in*)
Sleeve seam, 30.5cm (*12in*)

The figures in brackets [ ] refer to the
94/101.5cm (*37/40in*) size only

Tension

4½ shells and 16 rows to 10cm (*3.9in*) over
patt worked on No.2.50 (ISR) crochet hook

Note

It is easier to work with Minuit Lurex if the
ball of yarn is first placed on a central spool.
This can be done by rolling up a piece of
card, about 12.5cm (*5in*) square and
securing the end with sticky tape

Jacket

Using No.2.50 (ISR) crochet hook make

90[99]ch and beg at neck edge.

Base row Into 3rd ch from hook work 1dc, 1dc into each ch to end. Turn. 89[98]dc.

1st inc row 1ch to count as first dc, 1dc into each of next 7dc, *2dc into next dc, 1dc into each of next 8dc, rep from * to end, working last dc into turning ch. Turn. 98[107]dc.

Next row 1ch, *1dc into next dc, rep from * to end. Turn.

2nd inc row (buttonhole row) 1ch, 1dc into each of next 2dc, 3ch, miss 3dc, 1dc into each of next 2dc, *2dc into next dc, 1dc into each of next 9[10]dc, rep from * to end. Turn. 107[116]dc.

Next row 1ch, 1dc into each dc to end, working 3dc into 3ch loop of previous row. Turn.

3rd inc row 1ch to count as first dc, 1dc into next 7dc, *2dc into next dc, 1dc into each of next 10[11]dc, rep from * to end. Turn. 116[125]dc.

Next row 1ch, 1dc into each dc to end. Turn. Commence lace patt.

Base row 1ch to count as first dc, 1dc into each of next 6dc for right front border, *5ch, miss 2dc, 1dc into next dc, rep from * to last 7dc, turn and leave these 7dc for left front border. 34[37] 5ch loops.

1st row 1ch, *into next 5ch loop work (2dc, 3ch, ss into last dc to form picot, 3dc, 1 picot, 2dc) – called 1 shell –, ss into next dc, rep from * to end, working 1dc into last dc. Turn.

2nd row 7ch, 1dc into centre dc between first 2 picots, *5ch, 1dc into centre dc between 2 picots on next shell, rep from * to end, 3ch, 1dtr into last dc. Turn.

3rd row 1ch to count as first dc, into next 3ch loop work (1dc, 1 picot, 2dc), ss into next dc, *1 shell into next 5ch loop, ss into next dc, rep from * to end, ending with 2dc, 1 picot, 2dc into 7ch loop, 1dc into 4th of 7ch. Turn.

4th row 1ch to count as first dc, * 5ch, 1dc into centre dc between 2 picots on next shell, rep from * to end, 3ch, 1dtr into last dc. Turn. These 4 rows form patt, noting that on subsequent 1st patt rows the first shell will be worked into 3ch loop and last dc will be worked into 3rd of 5ch loop. Rep them once more, then first of them again.

Shape yoke

**1st inc row Patt 6[7] loops, (always counting ½ loops at ends of rows as 1 loop), (5ch, miss next picot and 2dc, 1dc into ss between shells, 5ch, 1dc between next 2 picots – called inc 1), patt 6[6] loops, inc 1, patt 7[8] loops, inc 1, patt 6[6] loops, inc 1, patt to end. 39[42] loops.

Patt 3 rows without shaping.

2nd inc row Work as given for 1st inc row, working 11[12] loops in centre back instead of 7[8] loops. 43[46] loops.

Patt 3 rows without shaping.

3rd inc row Patt 3[4] loops, *inc 1, patt 5 loops, rep from * ending last rep with 3[5] loops.

Patt 3 rows without shaping.

4th inc row Patt 3[5] loops, *inc 1, patt 5 loops, rep from * ending last rep with 3[5] loops.

Patt 3 rows without shaping.

5th inc row Patt 2[3] loops, *inc 1, patt 5 loops, rep from * ending last rep with 1[3] loops. 68[71] loops.

Patt 3 rows without shaping.

Divide for underarm

Next row Patt 12[13] loops, *work 15[18] ch, miss 11[12] shells, 1dc between next 2 picots, *, patt 19[20] loops, rep from * to * once more, patt to end. Turn.

Next row Patt 12[13] loops, *1dc into each of next 15[18]ch, *, patt 19[20] loops, rep from * to * once more, patt to end. Turn.

Next row Patt 12[13] loops, *5ch, miss first of 15[18]dc at underarm, 1dc into next dc, (5ch, miss 3dc, 1dc into next dc) 3[4] times, 5ch, 1dc between next 2 picots, *, patt 18[19] loops, rep from * to * once more, patt to end. Turn. 51[56] loops.

Keeping patt correct, cont without shaping until 13[16] picot rows in all have been worked from underarm. Fasten off.

Sleeves

Using No.2.50 (ISR) hook and with WS of work facing, rejoin yarn to centre dc at 15 underarm dc for 1st size and between 2 centre dc of 18dc for 2nd size.

Next row (5ch, miss 3dc, 1dc into next dc) once [twice], 5ch, 1dc into next dc, (5ch, 1dc between next 2 picots) 11[12] times, 5ch, 1dc into next dc before underarm, (5ch, miss 3dc, 1dc into next dc) twice. Turn. 16[18] loops.

Cont in patt until 14 picot rows in all have been worked from underarm, ending with a picot row.

Next row (inc) Patt 1 loop, inc 1 as given for yoke, patt 5[6] loops, inc 1, patt 6[7] loops, inc 1, patt to end. Turn. 19[21] loops.

Patt 7[9] more rows without shaping. Fasten off.

To make up

Do not press. Join sleeve seams.

Edging Using No.2.50 (ISR) hook and with WS of left front facing, rejoin yarn to 7dc at neck, 1ch, 1dc into each dc to end. Turn.

Next row 1ch, 1dc into each dc to end. Turn.

Rep this row until border, slightly stretched, fits down left front to lower edge. Fasten off. Work other side in same way. Sl st borders into place. With RS of work facing, rejoin yarn to right front at neck edge and work 1 row ss all round neck edge. Fasten off. Sew on button to correspond with buttonhole.

Lacy smock

Sizes
To fit 81.5/86.5cm *32/34in*) bust
Length from shoulder, 56cm (*22in*)

Tension
8tr and 4 rows to 9cm (*3½in*) over yoke patt
worked on No.7.00 (ISR) hook

Materials
6 × 50grm balls Claude by 3 Suisses
One No.7.00 (ISR) crochet hook
Motif to sew on (optional)

Back
Using No.7.00 (ISR) hook make 10ch.
1st row Into 4th ch from hook work 1tr, 1tr
into each ch to end. Turn. 8tr.
2nd row 3ch to count as first tr, miss first
tr, 1tr into each tr to end, finishing 1tr into
3rd of 3ch. Turn.
Rep last row once more. Fasten off.
Make a second piece in the same way, but
do not fasten off.
4th row Patt across second piece, 12ch,
then patt across first piece. Turn.
5th row 3ch, miss first tr, 1tr into each of
next 7tr, 1tr into each of next 12ch, 1tr into
each of next 8tr. Turn. 28tr.
6th row 3ch, miss first tr, 1tr into every tr
to end. Turn.
7th row 3ch, 1tr into first tr – 1tr increased
–, 1tr into every tr to last tr, 2tr into 3rd of
3ch. Turn. 30 sts.
8th row 4ch to count as first dtr, 1dtr into
first tr, 1dtr into every tr to last tr, 2dtr
into 4th of 4ch. Turn. 32 sts.
9th row 4ch, miss first 2dtr, *3dtr into next
dtr, miss next 2dtr, rep from * 8 times more,
3dtr into next dtr, miss next dtr, 1dtr into
4th of 4ch. Turn.
10th row 5ch, 1dtr into sp between first
dtr and gr of 3dtr, *1ch, 1dtr into centre dtr
of next gr, 1ch, 1dtr into next sp between
grs, rep from * ending with 1dtr between
last gr and turning ch, 1ch, 1dtr into 4th of
5ch. Turn.
11th row 5ch, *1dtr into next 1ch sp, 1ch,
rep from * finishing 1dtr into last 1ch sp,
1dtr into 4th of 5ch. Turn.
12th and 13th rows As 11th. 26dtr.
14th row 5ch, 1dtr into first 1ch sp, *(1dtr,
1ch, 1dtr) into next sp, (1ch, 1dtr into next
sp) twice, 1ch, rep from * to end. Turn.
15th row 5ch, 1dtr into first sp, * 1ch, 1dtr
into next sp, rep from * to end. Turn.
16th row 5ch, *(1dtr into next sp, 1ch)
twice, (1dtr, 1ch, 1dtr) into next sp, 1ch,
rep from * finishing (1dtr into next sp, 1ch)

twice, 1dtr into last sp. Turn.
17th row As 15th. Fasten off.

Front
Using No.7.00 (ISR) hook make 10ch.
Working an extra row in each, make 2
pieces as given for back. Do not fasten off
second piece.
5th row As 4th row of back.
6th row As 5th row of back. 28tr.
7th to 10th rows As 7th to 10th rows back.
11th row 5ch, 1dtr into next dtr, * 1ch, 3dtr
into next dtr, miss next dtr, rep from * 8
times more, 1ch, 3dtr into next dtr, 1ch, 1dtr
into next dtr, 1ch, 1dtr into 4th of 5ch. Turn.
12th row 5ch, 1dtr into first 1ch sp, *1ch,
1dtr into next 1ch sp, 1ch, 1dtr into centre
dtr of next gr, rep from * 9 times more,
(1ch, 1dtr into next sp) twice, 1ch, 1dtr into
4th of 5ch. Turn.
13th row As 11th row of back.
14th to 17th rows As 14th to 17th rows of
back. Fasten off.

Armhole frills
Join shoulder seams. Using No.7.00 (ISR)
hook and with RS of work facing, join yarn
to 8th row (first row of dtr), 3ch, 2tr into
this row end, 2tr into each row end round
armhole, 3tr into last row end (first row of
dtr on other side of garment). Turn.
Next row 4ch, (1tr, 1ch) into each sp
between tr of previous row, ending with 1tr
into 3rd of 3ch. Turn.
Next row 4ch, 1tr into first 1ch sp, 1ch,
(1tr, 1ch) twice into each 1ch sp, finishing
(1tr, 1ch, 1tr) in to last sp. Fasten off.

To make up
Join side seams.
Neck edging Using No.7.00 (ISR) hook
and with RS of work facing, join yarn to
corner at beg of back, *3ch, miss 1 sp
between tr, ss into next sp between tr, rep
from * along back, 3ch, ss into end of row,
**3ch, ss into end of next row, rep from **
up side, then cont in the same way across
front and up other side, ending with ss into
same place that yarn was joined. Fasten off.
Lower edging Using No.7.00 (ISR) hook
and with RS of work facing, join yarn to
one side, *5ch, miss 1dtr, ss into next dtr,
rep from * all round, ending with ss into
same place that yarn was joined.
Next row Ss to centre of first sp, *6ch, ss
into next sp, rep from * round, ending
with ss to first ch of first sp. Fasten off. Sew
motif on yoke if required.

Carry-all carpet bag

Size
35.5cm (*14in*) square

Tension
10 sts and 5 rows to 10cm (*3.9in*) over tr worked on No.6.00 (ISR) crochet hook

Materials
Pingouin uncut Tapis rug yarn
5 × 50grm balls of main shade, A
2 balls each of contrast colours, B, D and E
1 ball of contrast colour, C
One No.6.00 (ISR) crochet hook 2 buttons

Bag
Using No.6.00 (ISR) hook and E, make 5ch. Join with a ss to first ch to form circle.
1st round Using E, 3ch, 1tr into circle, 2ch, work (2tr into circle, 2ch) 3 times. Join with a ss to 3rd of first 3ch.
2nd round Using E, 2ch, *work (2tr, 2ch, 2tr) into 2ch sp to form corner, 1ch, rep from * 3 times more, omitting last 1ch. Join with a ss to first of first 2ch. Break off E.
3rd round Join in D with a ss to any 2ch sp, 3ch, 1tr into same sp, 1ch, 2tr into next 1ch sp, 1ch, *(2tr, 2ch, 2tr) into next 2ch sp, 1ch, 2tr into next 1ch sp, 1ch, rep from * twice more, 2tr into same ch sp as beg of round, 2ch. Join with a ss to 3rd of first 3ch. Break off D.
4th round Rejoin D with a ss to any 2ch sp, 3ch, 1tr into same sp, *1ch, (2tr into next 1ch sp, 1ch) twice, (2tr, 2ch, 2tr) into next 2ch sp, rep from * twice more, 1ch, (2tr in to next 1ch sp, 1ch) twice, 2tr into same ch sp as beg of round, 2ch. Join with a ss to 3rd of first 3ch. Break off D.
5th round Join in C with a ss to any 2ch sp, 3ch, 1tr into same sp, *1ch, (2tr into next 1ch sp, 1ch) 3 times, (2tr, 2ch, 2tr) into next 2ch sp, rep from * twice more, 1ch, (2tr into next 1ch sp, 1ch) 3 times, 2tr into same ch sp as beg of round, 2ch. Join with a ss to 3rd of first 3ch. Break off C.
Cont in this way working 1 more block of 2tr and 1ch on each side of every round, work 1 more round C, 2 rounds B, 1 round E and 1 round A. Fasten off.
Make another square in same way.

Strap and gusset
Using No.6.00 (ISR) hook and A, make 10ch.
1st row Into 4th ch from hook work 1tr, 1tr into each ch to end. 8tr.
2nd row 3ch to count as first tr, miss first tr, 1tr into each of next 6tr, 1tr into 3rd of first 3ch.
Rep 2nd row until work measures 167.5cm (*66in*) from beg. Fasten off.

To make up
Press each piece lightly under a damp cloth with a warm iron. Join strap into a circle. With WS facing, pin in place round 3 edges of both squares to form gusset. Using No.6.00 (ISR) hook and D, work 1 round dc along edge of strap and square, working through both thicknesses, then cont along edge of strap which forms handle. Work round other side in same way. Using D, work 1 row dc along top edges of bag.
Button loop Using No.6.00 (ISR) hook and A, make 15ch.
Next row Into 6th ch from hook work 1dc, 1dc into each of next 9ch, ss into last ch. Fasten off.
Sew one button to each side of top edge of bag. Fasten with button loop.

Leather trim string-bag

Size
Width across top, 40.5cm (*16in*)
Depth, 35.5cm (*14in*)

Tension
4 ch loops and 6 rounds to 10cm (*3.9in*) over patt worked on No.3.50 (ISR) crochet hook

Materials
1 ball thin parcel string
One No.3.50 (ISR) crochet hook
1 strip of leather, 7.5cm × 89cm (*3in × 35in*), for binding on bag opening
2 strips, each 4cm × 89cm (*1½in × 35in*), for supporting straps
2 strips, each 4cm × 81.5cm (*1½in × 32in*), for strap facings
2 strips, each 4cm × 66cm (*1½in × 26in*), for handles
2 strips, each 4cm × 58.5cm (*1½in × 23in*), for handle facings
Matching buttonhole twist
4 D rings, each 5cm (*2in*) in diameter
Paper clips

Bag
Using No.3.50 (ISR) hook make 100ch. Join with a ss into first ch to form a circle.
1st round 10ch, miss next 4ch, *1dc into next ch, 9ch, miss next 4ch, rep from * to end. Join with a ss into first 10ch. 20 ch loops.
2nd round 10ch, 1dc into centre ch of next loop, *9ch, 1dc into centre ch of next loop, rep from * to last loop, 5ch. Join with a ss into 6th ch of first loop.
3rd round 10ch, *1dc into centre ch of next loop, 9ch, rep from * to end. Join with a ss into first of 10ch.
4th round 10ch, 1dc into next loop, (9ch, 1dc into next loop) twice, 9ch, 1dc into next dc, (9ch, 1dc into next loop) 11 times, 9ch, 1dc into next dc, (9ch, 1dc into next loop) 6 times, 5ch. Join with a ss into first of 10ch. 2 loops inc.
5th round As 3rd.
6th to 7th rounds As 2nd to 3rd.
8th round 10ch, 1dc into next loop, (9ch, 1dc into next loop) 3 times, 9ch, 1dc into next dc, (9ch, 1dc in to next loop) 11 times, 9ch, 1dc into next dc, (9ch, 1dc into next loop) 7 times, 5ch. Join with a ss into first of 10ch. 2 loops inc.
Cont inc 2 loops in this way on every foll 4th round twice. 28 loops.
Patt 5 rounds without shaping.
Next round 9ch, *1dc into next loop, 5ch, rep from * to end. Join with a ss into 5th of 9ch.
Fasten off.

To make up
Fold bag in half so that increases are at side edge.
Join lower edge Using No.3.50 (ISR) hook and with RS of work facing, cont in dc across lower edge of bag, working through double thickness of foundation chain.
Leather trimming and handles Note that strips may be joined if necessary. It is preferable to make joins where they will be hidden by another strap where possible.
Binding round opening Overlap short ends by 2.5cm (*1in*). Glue and stitch. Fold strip in half and place over rim of bag so enclosing it by approx 2.5cm (*1in*). Hold edges of strip tog with paper clips and stitch tog all round bag, approx 0.5cm (*¼in*) from edges, working through crochet loops where they occur.
Supporting straps Glue leather over straight edge of D rings at either end of straps turning over approx 2cm (*¾in*) to do so at each end. Glue facings in position on back of strap to cover joins. Place straps round bag, positioning the first strap where the crochet rounds are joined and the other strap the same distance from the opposite edge. Stitch the straps to the bag round all edges, 0.5cm (*¼in*) from edge and stitching through crochet loops and rim binding.
Handles Glue ends of handles over curved edge of D rings in same way as given for straps. Glue facings to back. Stitch all round straps, 0.5cm (*¼in*) from edge.

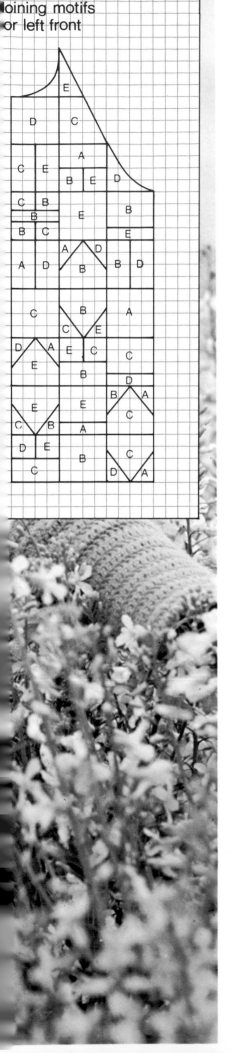

Spring time cardigan in shades of brown

Sizes
To fit 86.5[91.5:96.5:101.5]cm (*34*[*36:38: 40*]*in*) bust/chest
Length to shoulder, 68.5[68.5:76:76]cm (*27*[*27:30:30*]*in*)
Sleeve seam, 46[46:51:51]cm (*18*[*18:20:20*]*in*)
The figures in brackets [ ] refer to the 91.5 (*36*), 96.5 (*38*) and 101.5cm (*40in*) sizes respectively

Tension
18 sts and 9 rows to 10cm (*3.9in*) over tr worked on No.3.50 (ISR) crochet hook

Materials
11[12:12:13] × 50grm balls Grosvenor Double Knitting by 3 Suisses in main shade, A
2[2:2:2] balls each of contrast colours, B and C
1[1:1:2] balls of contrast colour, D
1[2:2:3] balls of contrast colour, E
One No.3.50 [ISR] crochet hook
65[65:70:70]cm (*26*[*26:28:28*]*in*) open ended zip fastener

Back
Using No.3.50 (ISR) hook and A, make 82 [88:94:96]ch.
1st row Into 4th ch from hook work 1tr, 1tr into each ch to end. Turn. 80[86:92:94]tr.
2nd row 3ch to count as first tr, miss first tr, 1tr into each tr to end. Turn.
Rep 2nd row 40[40:49:49] times more
Shape raglan armholes
Next row Ss across first 6[6:7:7] tr, 1tr into each tr to last 6[6:7:7]tr, turn.
Next row 3ch to count as first tr, yrh, insert hook into next tr, yrh and draw through loop, yrh and draw through 2 loops

on hook, yrh and insert hook into next tr, yrh and draw through loop, yrh and draw through 2 loops on hook, yrh and draw through 3 loops on hook – called dec 1 –, 1tr into each tr to last 3tr, dec 1, 1tr into last tr. Turn.
Rep last row 19[19:21:21] times more. Fasten off.

Sleeves
Using No.3.50 (ISR) hook and A, make 40[40:49:49]ch. Work 1st row as given for back. 38[38:47:47]tr.
1st and 2nd sizes only
Work 2 rows tr.
4th row 3ch, 2tr into next tr – called inc 1 –, 1tr into each tr to last 2tr, inc 1, 1tr into last tr.
Turn.
Work 2 rows tr without shaping, Cont inc in this way on next and every foll 3rd row until 34 rows have been worked from beg, then inc in same way on every foll 2nd row 5 times in all. 70[70]tr.
3rd and 4th sizes only
Work 4 rows tr. Inc as given for 1st and 2nd sizes on next and every foll 4th row until 21 rows have been worked from beg, then inc in same way on every foll 3rd row until there are 77[77]tr.

All sizes
Shape raglans
Next row Ss across first 6[6:7:7] tr, 3ch, 1tr into each tr to last 6[6:7:7] tr, turn.
Dec one st at each end of every row until 30[30:31:31]tr rem.
Next row 3ch, dec 1, 1tr into each of next 9tr, dec 1, 1tr into each of next 2[2:3:3]tr, dec 1, 1tr into each of next 9tr, dec 1, 1tr into last tr. Turn.

Next row 3ch, dec 1, 1tr into each of next 7tr, dec 1, 1tr into each of next 2[2:3:3]tr, dec 1, 1tr into each of next 7tr, dec 1, 1tr into last tr. Turn.
Cont dec in this way on next 4 rows. 6[6:7:7]tr. Fasten off.

Left and right fronts
Work motifs for fronts, noting that colours may be varied as required and should be twisted at back of work when changing colours.
1st motif
Using A, make 16[16:18:18]ch.
1st row Into 4th ch from hook work 1tr, 1tr into each ch to end. Turn. 14[14:16:16]tr.
2nd row 3ch to count as first tr, miss first tr, 1tr into each tr to end. Turn.
Rep 2nd row 5[5:6:6] times more. Fasten off and darn in ends. Work 1 more motif in same way using A, then 2 motifs each in B, C, D and E. 10 motifs, 5 for each front.
2nd motif
Using A, work first 2 rows as given for last motif. Break off A. Join in E. Complete as given for 1st motif. Work 1 more motif in same way, then 2 more using D and C and 2 more using E and B. 6 motifs, 3 for each front.
3rd motif
Using B, make 7[7:8:8]ch, join in D and make 9[9:10:10]ch.
1st row Using D, into 4th ch from hook work 1tr, 1tr into each of next 5[5:6:6]ch working last 2 loops of last tr with B – called 1trNc –, using B, work 1tr into each ch to end. Turn. 7[7:8:8]tr each in D and B.
2nd row Using B, 3ch to count as first tr, 1tr into each of next 6[6:7:7]tr, putting B to front of work and D to back under hook to work 1trNc with D on last tr, using D, work 1tr into each tr to end. Turn.
3rd row Using D, 3ch, work 1tr into each of next 6[6:7:7]tr, keeping yarn at back of work and working 1trNc with B on last tr, using B, work 1tr into each tr to end. Turn.
Rep 2nd and 3rd rows twice more, then 2nd row 0[0:1:1] times more. Fasten off and darn in ends. Work 1 more motif in same way, then 2 motifs using A and D and 2 using C and E. 6 motifs, 3 for each front.
4th motif
Using B and C, work first 3 rows as given for 3rd motif.
4th row Using B, 3ch, 1tr into each tr to end. Turn.
5th row Using B, 3ch, 1tr into each of next 6[6:7:7]tr, keeping yarn at back of work join in C and work 1trNc on last tr, using C, 1tr into each tr to end. Turn.
6th row Using C, 3ch, 1tr into each of next 6[6:7:7]tr, putting C to front of work and B under hook to work 1trNc with B on last tr, using B, 1tr into each tr to end. Turn.

7th row As 5th.
Rep 6th row 0[0:1:1] times more. Fasten off and darn in ends. Work 1 more motif.
5th motif
Using B, work first 3 rows as given for 1st motif, joining in E and working 1trNc on last tr. Break off B.
4th row Using E, 3ch, work 1tr into each of next 6[6:7:7]tr, join in C and work 1trNc on last tr, using C, 1tr into each tr to end. Turn.
5th row Using C, 3ch, work 1tr into each of next 6[6:7:7]tr, 1trNc with C on last tr using E, 1tr into each tr to end. Turn.
Rep 4th and 5th row once more, then 4th row 0[0:1:1] times more. Fasten off and darn in ends. Work 1 more motif in same way, then 2 more using C, E and D and 2 more using A, B and E. 6 motifs, 3 for each front.
6th motif
Using E, make 7[7:8:8]ch, join in D and make 9[9:10:10]ch.
1st row Using D, into 4th ch from hook work 1tr, 1tr into each of next 4[4:5:5]ch, keeping yarn at back of work join in C and work 1trNc on last tr, using C, 1tr into each of next 2ch, keeping yarn at back of work join in E and work 1trNc on last tr, using E, 1tr into each of next 6[6:7:7]ch. Turn.
2nd row Using E, 3ch, 1tr into each of next 4[4:5:5]tr, putting E to front of work and C to back under hook and working 1trNc with C on last tr, using C, 1tr into each of next 4tr, putting C to front of work and D to back under hook and working 1trNc with D on last tr, using D, 1tr into each tr to end. Turn.
3rd row Changing colours as for 1st row, using D, 3ch, 1tr into each of next 3[3:4:4]tr, using C, 1tr into each of next 6tr, using E, 1tr into each tr to end. Turn.
4th row Changing colours as for 2nd row, using E, 3ch, 1tr into each of next 2[2:3:3]tr, using C, 1tr into each of next 8tr, using D, 1tr into each tr to end. Turn.
5th row Changing colours as for 1st row, using D, 3ch, 1tr into next tr, using C, 1tr into each of next 10 tr, using E, 1tr into each tr to end. Turn.
6th row Changing colours as for 2nd row, using E, 3ch, 1tr into each of next 0[0:1:1]tr, using C, 1tr into each of next 12tr, using D, 1tr into each tr to end. Turn.
7th row Using C, 3ch, 1tr into each tr to end. Turn.
Rep 7th row 0[0:1:1] times more. Fasten off and darn in ends. Work 1 more motif in same way, then 2 using B, A and C, 2 using E, C and B, 2 using A, D and B, 2 using B, C and E and 2 using D, A and E. 12 motifs making 6 diamond shapes, 3 for each front.
Quarter raglan motif
Using D, make 10[10:12:12]ch. Work 1st row as given for 1st motif. 8[8:9:9]tr.
2nd row 3ch, dec 1, 1tr into each tr to end

Turn.
3rd row 3ch, 1tr into each tr to last 3tr, dec 1, 1tr into last tr. Turn.
Rep 2nd and 3rd rows twice more, then 2nd row 0[0:1:1] times more. Fasten off. Make another quarter motif in same way.
Three-quarter raglan motif
Using C, make 16[16:18:18]ch. Work 1st row as given for 1st motif. 14[14:16:16]tr.
2nd row 3ch, 1tr into next tr, dec 1, 1tr into each tr to end. Turn.
3rd row 3ch, 1tr into each tr to last 4tr, dec 1, 1tr into each of last 2tr. Turn.
Rep 2nd and 3rd rows twice more. 8[8:9:9]tr. Fasten off.
Neck motif
Using E, make 16[16:18:18]ch.
1st row Into 4th ch from hook work 1tr, 1tr into each ch to last 4ch, dec 2 working over next 3ch as given for dec 1, 1tr into last ch. Turn
2nd row 3ch, dec 2, 1tr into each tr to end. Turn.
3rd row 3ch, 1tr into each tr to last 4tr, dec 2, 1tr into last tr. Turn.
Rep 2nd and 3rd rows once more, then 2nd row once more. Fasten off.

To make up
Press each piece under a damp cloth with a warm iron. Sew motifs tog with cast off edge to cast on edge, with exception of 6th motif which must be sewn on cast on edges tog to form diamond shape. Join 3 motifs, arranging as required or as shown in diagram, to form one row. Join 5 more rows in same way, then join these 6 rows tog to form one front to underarm. Join 2 motifs working from front edge for 7th row then join quarter raglan motif for armhole edge. Join one motif for front edge with three-quarter raglan motif for armhole edge for 8th row, then join neck motif to raglan edge of armhole, leaving 9tr at neck edge free for 9th row. Join other front in same way, reversing motifs.
Collar Using No.3.50 (ISR) hook, A and with RS of work facing, work 86[86:90:90] dc round neck edge. Work 1 row tr, dec one st at each side of sleeve, (4 dec). Cont dec in same way, work 1 row dc and 1 row tr. Work 2[2:3:3] rows dc without shaping. Fasten off.
Lower edge Using No.3.50 (ISR) hook, A and with RS of front facing, work 2[2:3:3] rows tr along lower edge for hem. Fasten off. Work other front in same way.
Front edges Using No.3.50 (ISR) hook, A and with RS of work facing, work 3 rows dc along each front edge. Fasten off.
Join raglan, side and sleeve seams. Turn up hem at lower edge and sl st down. Turn up 2[2:3:3] rows tr at cuffs and sl st down. Sew in zip. Press seams

Glamorous glitter caps for sophisticated parties

Size
To fit an average adult head

Tension
16 sts and 7 rows to 5cm (*2in*) over tr worked on No.1.00 (ISR) crochet hook

Materials
1 × 20grm ball Wendy Minuit Lurex
One No.1.00 (ISR) crochet hook
Shirring elastic for edging

Hat
One style to make in two colours.
Using No.1.00 (ISR) hook, make 5ch and beg in centre of crown. Join with a ss to first ch to form circle.

1st round 1ch to count as first dc, 9dc into circle. Join with a ss to first ch. 10dc.

2nd round 3ch to count as first tr, 2tr into next dc, (2ch, 1tr into next dc, 2tr into next dc) 4 times, 2ch. Join with a ss to 3rd of first 3ch.

3rd round 3ch, 1tr into same place, 1tr into next tr, 2tr into next tr, (3ch, 2tr into next tr – called inc 1 –, 1tr into next tr, inc 1) 4 times, 3ch. Join with a ss to 3rd of first 3ch.

4th round 3ch, 1tr into same place, 1tr into each of next 3tr, inc 1, (4ch, inc 1, 1tr into each of next 3tr, inc 1) 4 times, 4ch. Join with a ss to 3rd of first 3ch.

5th round 3ch, 1tr into same place, (1tr into each of next 2tr, inc 1) twice, *4ch, inc 1, (1tr into each of next 2tr, inc 1) twice, rep from * 3 times more, 4ch. Join with a ss to 3rd of first 3ch.

6th round 3ch, 1tr into same place, 1tr into each of next 3tr, (inc 1) twice, 1tr into each of next 3tr, inc 1, *4ch, (inc 1, 1tr into each of next 3tr, inc 1) twice, rep from * 3 times more, 4ch. Join with a ss to 3rd of first 3ch.
Work 2 more rounds in same way, inc at beg and end of each block of tr and in 2 centre sts.

9th round 3ch, 1tr into same place, 1tr into each of next 20tr, inc 1, (4ch, inc 1, 1tr into each of next 20tr, inc 1) 4 times, 4ch. Join with a ss to 3rd of first 3ch.

10th round As 9th, working 22tr between inc. Join with a ss to 3rd of first 3ch. 130tr.
Work 3 rounds without inc as last round.

14th round 8ch, miss first 4tr, 1tr into next tr, (5ch, miss next 4tr, 1tr into next tr) 4 times, *5ch, 1tr into next tr, (5ch, miss next 4tr, 1tr into next tr) 5 times, rep from * to end, 5ch. Join with a ss to 3rd of first 8ch. 30 5ch sp.

15th round 8ch, 1tr into next tr, *5ch, 1tr into next tr, rep from * to end, 5ch. Join with a ss to 3rd of first 8ch.
Rep last round 4 times more.

To make up
Join elastic to fit head and holding elastic behind work, cont as foll:

20th round 1ch, 4dc into 5ch sp, working over elastic, 1dc into tr, *5dc into 5ch sp, 1dc into tr, rep from * to end. Join with a ss to first ch. Fasten off.

Free & easy beach bag

Size
Approx 61cm (*24in*) long

Materials
2 × 50grm balls Twilley's Stalite
One No.4.00 (ISR) crochet hook

Beach bag
Using No.4.00 (ISR) hook make 4ch.
Join with a ss into first ch to form a circle.
1st round 1ch to count as first dc, 7dc into circle. Join with a ss into first ch.
2nd round *1ch, 1dc into next dc, rep from * all round. Do not join any rounds from this point.
3rd round *2ch, 1dc into next 1ch sp, rep from * all round

4th round *3ch, 1dc into next 2ch sp, rep from * all round. Eight 3ch sp.
5th round *3ch, 1dc into next 3ch sp, 3ch, 1dc into same sp, rep from * all round. Sixteen 3ch sp.
6th-8th rounds *3ch, 1dc into next 3ch sp, rep from * all round.
9th round *5ch, 1dc into next 3ch sp, rep from * all round.
10th round *(5ch and 1dc) twice into next 5ch sp, 5ch, 1dc into next 5ch sp, rep from * all round. Twenty-four 5ch sp.
11th-14th rounds *5ch, 1dc into next 5ch sp, rep from * all round.
15th round As 10th. Thirty-six 5ch sp.
16th-19th rounds As 11th.
20th round *(5ch, 1dc into next 5ch sp)

8 times, (5ch, 1dc into next sp) twice, rep from * all round. Forty 5ch sp.
Rep 11th round until work measures 61cm (*24in*) or length required from beg.
Next round *2dc into next 5ch sp, 4ch, ss into first ch just worked, 2dc into same 5ch sp, rep from * all round. Join with a ss into first dc.
Fasten off.

To make up
Using 4 strands of yarn tog, make a twisted cord approx 244cm (96in) long. Thread through ch sp in last round and join ends of cord.
Make a thick tassel about 15cm (6in) long and attach to the bottom of the bag

Super tote bag

Size
30.5cm× 30.5cm (*12in*× *12in*) square

Tension
21 sts and 14 rows to 10cm (*3.9in*) over tr worked on No.2.50 (ISR) crochet hook; each square motif measures 20.5cm× 20.5cm (*8in*× *8in*)

Materials
4× 25grm balls Robin Tricel Nylon Perle 4 ply in main shade, A *or* oddments of 14 contrast colours
One No.2.50 (ISR) crochet hook
One button
0.35 metres (*⅜ yard*) of buckram, 91.5cm (*36in*) wide, optional
0.35 metres (*⅜ yard*) of lining fabric, 91.5cm (*36in*) wide, optional

Square motif
Using No.2.50 (ISR) hook and any colour, make 6ch. Join with a ss to first ch to form circle.

1st round 3ch to count as first tr, 2tr, 3ch, 3tr into circle, *1ch, 3tr, 3ch, 3tr into circle, rep from * twice more, 1ch. Join with a ss to 3rd of first 3ch. Break off yarn.

2nd round Join any colour to first 3ch sp of last round 3ch, 2tr, 3ch, 3tr into first 3ch sp, *1ch, 3tr into 1ch sp, 1ch, 3tr, 3ch, 3tr into next 3ch sp, rep from * twice more, 1ch, 3tr into 1ch sp, 1ch. Join with a ss to 3rd of first 3ch. Break off yarn.

Cont as given for last round, inc one ch sp at either side of corners, using colours as required, until 14 rounds in all have been worked. Fasten off.

Make one more square motif in same way.

Half motif
Using No.2.50 (ISR) hook and any colour, make 6ch. Join with a ss to first ch to form circle.

1st row 5ch to count as first tr and 2ch sp, 3tr, 3ch, 3tr into circle, 2ch, 1tr into circle. Break off yarn.

2nd row Join next colour to 3rd of 5ch at beg of last row, 5ch, 3tr into first 2ch sp, 1ch, (3tr, 3ch, 3tr) into 3ch sp, 1ch, (3tr, 2ch, 1tr) into last 2ch sp. Break off yarn.

3rd row Join next colour to 3rd of 5ch at beg of last row, 5ch, 3tr into first 2ch sp, 1ch, 3tr into 1ch sp, 1ch, (3tr, 3ch, 3tr) into 3ch sp, 1ch, 3tr into 1ch sp, (3tr, 2ch, 1tr) into last 2ch sp. Break off yarn.

Cont in this way, inc one ch sp at either side of centre and working each row in different colour, until 14 rows in all have been worked. Fasten off.

Make 4 more half motifs in same way.

To make up
Darn in all ends. Join motifs as shown in diagram.

Flap edge Using No.2.50 (ISR) hook, any colour and with RS of work facing, beg at corner sp of square motif, work 3ch, 1tr, 1htr, 1dc into this sp, *1dc, 1htr, 3tr, 1htr, 1dc into next ch sp, *, rep from * to * down flap to point, 1dc, 1htr, 2tr, 10ch for button loop, ss into last tr, 1tr, 1htr, 1dc into corner, rep from * to * up other side of flap, working 1dc, 1htr, 2tr into last st at corner sp. Fasten off.

Lining Cut interlining and lining to fit bag, allowing 1.5cm (*½in*) turnings on lining. Tack round edges on lining and interlining, folding 1.5cm (*½in*) hem all round. Stitch interlining and lining to bag. Remove tacking. With RS of bag tog, join side seams. Turn bag RS out. Sew on button. Make a plait approx 129.5cm (*51in*) long, using all colours tog. Sew plait in position down side seams, leaving tassels hanging free at lower edge.

A warm and beautiful shawl to treasure forever

Size
122cm (*48in*) diameter

Tension
First 5 rows equal 14cm (*5½in*) diameter worked on No.2.50 (ISR) crochet hook

Materials
14 × 20grm balls Lister Baby Easy Wash Courtelle Nylon 3 ply
One No.2.50 (ISR) crochet hook

Shawl
Using No.2.50 (ISR) hook make 8ch. Join with a ss to first ch to form circle.
1st round 2ch to count as first dc, work 15dc into circle. 16 sts. Join with a ss to 2nd of first 2ch.
2nd round 4ch to count as first dtr, 1dtr into next dc, *4ch, 1dtr into each of next 2dc, rep from * to end, 4ch. Join with a ss to 4th of first 4ch.
3rd round Ss into next dtr and into first 4ch sp, 4ch, 5dtr into same sp, *3ch, 6dtr into next sp, rep from * to end, 3ch. Join with a ss to 4th of first 4ch.
4th round 4ch, 1dtr into same place as last ss, *1dtr into each of next 4dtr, 2dtr into next dtr, 4ch, 2dtr into next dtr, rep from * to end, omitting 2dtr at end of last rep. Join with a ss to 4th of first 4ch.
5th round 4ch, 1dtr into each of next 7dtr leaving last loop of each dtr on hook, yrh and draw through all loops on hook, *8ch, 1dc into next sp, 8ch, 1dtr into each of next 8dtr leaving last loop of each dtr on hook, yrh and draw through all loops on hook – called 1cl –, rep from * ending with 8ch, 1dc into next sp, 8ch. Join with a ss to top of first 1cl.

6th round Ss into each of next 4ch, 1dc into loop, *9ch, 1dc into next loop, rep from * ending with 9ch. Join with a ss to first dc.
7th round Ss into each of next 3ch, 4ch, 4dtr into same loop, *5ch, 5dtr into next loop, rep from * ending 5ch. Join with a ss to 4th of first 4ch.
8th round 1dc into same place as last ss, 1dc into each of next 4dtr, *5dc into next sp, 1dc into each of next 5dtr, rep from * ending with 5dc into last sp. Join with a ss to first dc.
9th round 5ch, 1tr tr, 4ch and 2tr tr into same place as last ss, *miss 4dc, 2tr tr, 4ch and 2tr tr into next dc, rep from * to end. Join with a ss to 5th of first 5ch.
10th round 1dc into same place as last ss, 1dc into next tr tr, *4dc into next sp, 1dc into each of next 4tr tr, rep from * ending with 4dc into last sp, 1dc into each of next 2tr tr. Join with a ss to first dc.
11th round 5ch, 1tr tr into same place as last ss, *miss 6dc, 2tr tr into next dc, 6ch, 2tr tr into next dc, rep from * omitting 2tr tr at end of last rep.
Join with a ss to 5th of first 5ch.
12th round 1dc into same place as last ss, 1dc into each of next 3tr tr, *6dc into next sp, 1dc into each of next 4tr tr, rep from * ending with 6dc into last sp. Join with a ss to first dc.
13th round 1dc into first dc, *5ch, miss 3dc, 1dc into next dc, rep from * to end. Join with a ss to first dc.
14th round Ss to centre of first loop, 5ch, 1tr into first loop, *1tr, 2ch and 1tr into next loop, rep from * to end. Join with a ss to 3rd of first 5ch.
15th, 16th and 17th rounds As 14th.
18th round 4ch, 5dtr into first loop, *miss

1 loop, 2ch, 6dtr into next loop, rep from * to end. Join with a ss into 4th of first 4ch.
19th round 4ch, 1dtr into same 4ch, 1dtr into each of next 4dtr, 2dtr into next dtr, *2ch, 2dtr into first of next 6dtr, 1dtr into each of next 4dtr, 2dtr into next dtr, rep from * to end. Join with a ss to 4th of first 4ch.
20th round 4ch, 1dtr into each of next 7dtr leaving last loop of each dtr on hook, yrh and draw through all loops on hook, *8ch, 1dc into next loop, 8ch, 1cl, rep from * ending with 8ch, 1dc into next loop, 8ch. Join with a ss to top of first 1cl.
21st round *6ch, 1dc into first loop, 6ch, 1dc into next loop, 6ch, 1dc into top of 1cl, rep from * to end.
22nd, 23rd and 24th rounds As 14th.
25th round As 18th.
26th round As 19th.
27th round As 20th.
28th round As 21st.
29th-35th rounds As 14th.
36th round As 18th.
37th round As 19th.
38th round As 20th.
39th round Ss into centre of first loop, 1dc into same loop, *7ch, 1dc into next loop, rep from * to end, 7ch.
Join with a ss to first dc.
40th round As 14th, working 6ch at beg and 3ch between tr.
41st-44th rounds As 40th.
45th round Ss into centre of first loop, 1dc into same loop, *5ch, 1dc into next loop, rep from * to end, 5ch.
Join with a ss to first dc.
46th round Ss into first loop, 3ch, 1tr, 2ch and 2tr into first loop, * 2tr, 2ch and 2tr into next loop, rep from * to end. Join with a ss to 3rd of first 3ch.
47th round Ss into first 2ch loop, 3ch, 1tr, 2ch and 2tr into same loop, *2tr, 2ch and 2tr into next loop, rep from * to end. Join with a ss to 3rd of first 3ch.
48th round Ss into first 2ch loop, 3ch, 1tr, 2ch and 2tr into same loop, *1ch, 2tr, 2ch and 2tr into next loop, rep from * to end, 1ch. Join with a ss to 3rd of first 3ch.
49th round As 48th.
50th round Ss into first 2ch loop, 3ch, 1tr, 2ch and 2tr into same loop, *2ch, 2tr, 2ch and 2tr into next loop, rep from * to end, 2ch. Join with a ss to 3rd of first 3ch.
51st and 52nd rounds As 50th.
53rd round Ss into first 2ch loop, 3ch, 1tr, 3ch and work 1dc into first ch to form picot and 2tr into same loop, *2ch, 2tr, 1 picot, 2tr into next loop, rep from * to end, 2ch. Join with a ss to 3rd of first 3ch.
Fasten off.

To make up
Do not press.
Darn in all ends.

Open-work angel top

Sizes
To fit 45.5[51]cm (*18[20]in*) chest
Length to centre back, 26.5[29]cm
(*10½[11½]in*)
Sleeve seam, 14[15]cm (*5½[6]in*)
The figures in brackets [ ] refer to the
51cm (*20in*) size only

Tension
24 sts and 24 rows to 10cm (*3.9in*) over dc
worked on No.3.50 (ISR) crochet hook

Materials
5[6]× 20grm balls Wendy Tricel Nylon
4 ply Crepe
One No.3.50 (ISR) crochet hook
One No.3.00 (ISR) crochet hook
7 small buttons
2 motifs, optional

Angel top
Using No.3.50 (ISR) hook make 117[125] ch
and work in one piece to underarm.
Base row Into 5th ch from hook work 4tr
leaving last loop of each st on hook, yrh and
draw through all loops – called 1cl –, *1ch,
miss 1ch, 1cl into next ch, rep from * to last
2ch, 1ch, miss 1ch, 1tr into last ch. Turn.
56[60]cl plus 1tr at each end.
1st row (RS) 4ch, miss first cl, *1tr into next
ch sp between cl, 1ch, rep from * to end,
1tr into 3rd of first 4ch. Turn.

2nd row 4ch, 1cl into first ch sp, 1ch, *1cl
into next ch sp, 1ch, rep from * ending 1ch,
1cl into last ch sp, 1ch, 1tr into 3rd of first
4ch. Turn.
The last 2 rows form patt. Rep these 2 rows
8[9] times more, then first of them again.
Shape waist
Next row 2ch, *(1dc into next ch sp, 1dc
into next tr) twice, insert hook into next ch
sp, yrh and draw loop through, insert hook
into next tr, yrh and draw loop through, yrh
and draw through all loops on hook – called
dec 1dc –, rep from * to last 2 sp and tr, 1dc
into ch sp, 1dc into tr, 1dc into last ch sp, 1dc
into 3rd of first 4ch. Turn. Work 4[6] rows dc.
Divide for armholes
Next row 2ch, 1dc into each of next
21[22]dc, turn.
Complete left back on these 22[23] sts.
Next row 2ch, dec 1dc, work in dc to end.
Turn.
Next row 2ch, work in dc to end. Turn.
Rep last 2 rows until 12 sts rem. Fasten off.
With RS of work facing, miss first 4[5]dc
for underarm, rejoin yarn to next dc, 2ch,
1dc into each of next 43[45]dc, turn.
Complete front on these 44[46] sts.
Next row 2ch, dec 1dc, work in dc to last
3dc, dec 1dc, 1dc into turning ch. Turn.
Next row 2ch, work in dc to end. Turn.
Rep last 2 rows until 30 sts rem, ending with
a WS row.

Shape neck
Next row 2ch, 1dc into each of next 8dc,
turn.
Dec 1dc at neck edge on every row, *at the
same time* dec 1dc at raglan edge as before
until all sts are worked off. Fasten off.
With RS of work facing, miss first 12dc for
centre neck, rejoin yarn to next dc, 2ch, 1dc
into each dc to end. Complete to match
first side, reversing shaping.
With RS of work facing, miss first 4[5]dc
for underarm, rejoin yarn to next dc, 2ch,
1dc into each dc to end. Turn. Complete to
match left back, reversing shaping.

Sleeves
Using No.3.50 (ISR) hook make 27[31] ch.
Work base row as given for skirt.
Next row (RS) 2ch, miss first ch sp, *1dc
into next cl, 1dc into next ch sp, rep from *
ending with 1dc into 3rd of first 4ch. Turn.
24[28]dc.
Cont in dc, inc 1dc at each end of every 8th
row until there are 30[34]dc. Cont without
shaping until sleeve measures 14[15]cm
(*5½[6]in*) from beg, ending with a WS row.
Shape top
Next row Ss over 2[3]dc, work in dc to
last 2[3]dc, turn.
Dec 1dc at each end of next and every alt
row until 4 sts rem. Fasten off.

Neckband
Join raglan seams. Using No.3.00 (ISR) hook
and with RS of work facing, work 61[65]dc
round neck edge. Turn.
Next row 4ch, *1cl into next dc, 1ch, miss
1dc, rep from * to end, ending with 1tr in
last dc. Fasten off.

Borders
Using No.3.00 (ISR) hook and with RS of
work facing, work 1 row dc along left back
edge, working 2dc into end of each cl row,
2dc into each 1st patt row and 1dc into each
dc row. Turn.
Next row (buttonhole row) 2ch, 1dc into
each of next 2dc, 2ch, miss 2dc, *1dc into
each of next 6dc, 2ch, miss 2dc, rep from *
5 times more, work in dc to end. Turn.
Next row Work in dc to end, working 2dc
into each 2ch buttonhole. Turn.
Work 2 rows dc. Fasten off.
Work button border in same way along
right back edge, omitting buttonholes.

To make up
Press dc sections only under a dry cloth with
a cool iron. Join sleeve seams. Press seams.
Sew on buttons. Sew on motifs to centre
front, if required. Using No.3.50 (ISR) hook
and 2 ends of yarn, make a crochet ch 61cm
(*24in*) long. Thread through neck to tie at
back. Make ch 40.5cm (*16in*) long in same
way for each sleeve.

Super sun-suit in pink and white

Sizes

To fit 51 [56]cm (20[22]in)
Angel top length to centre back, 15cm (6in)
The figures in brackets [ ] refer to the 56cm (22in) size only

Tension

20 sts and 14 rows to 10cm (3.9in) over patt worked on No.3.50 (ISR) crochet hook

Materials

3 × 50grm balls Twilley's Stalite
One No.3.50 (ISR) crochet hook
4 buttons for angel top
Waist length of elastic for pants

Angel top front yoke

Using No.3.50 (ISR) hook make 47[53]ch.
1st row Into 3rd ch from hook work 1dc, 1dc into each ch to end.
Turn. 46[52] sts.
2nd row 3ch to count as first tr, miss first st, 1tr into each dc to end.
Turn.
Shape neck
Next row 1ch to count as first dc, 1dc into each of next 17[19] sts, turn.
Next row 3ch to count as first tr, miss first 2 sts, 1tr into each st to end.
Turn.
Next row 1ch to count as first dc, 1dc into each st to last st, turn.
Rep last 2 rows once more, then work first of them again.
13[15] sts.
Shape shoulder
Next row Ss over first 4 sts, 1ch to count as first dc, 1dc into each of next 7[9] sts, turn.
Next row 1ch to count as first dc, 1dc into each of next 3 sts.
Fasten off.
Return to where sts were left, miss 10[12] sts in centre, rejoin yarn to rem sts and patt to end. Complete to match first side, reversing shapings.
Shape skirt
With RS of work facing, return to lower

edge of yoke and rejoin yarn.
1st row 3ch to count as first tr, miss next st, 2tr, 1ch and 2tr into next st, *miss next 3 sts, 2tr, 1ch and 2tr into next st, rep from * to last 3[1] sts, 1tr into last st.
Turn. 11[13] grs.
2nd row 3ch, *2tr, 1ch and 2tr into next 1ch sp, rep from * to end, finishing with 1tr into 3rd of 3ch. Turn.
3rd row Using separate length of yarn, make 5ch and leave for time being, 5ch, into 4th ch from hook work 2tr, 2ch and 2tr, *2tr, 2ch and 2tr into next 1ch sp, rep from * to end, miss last tr, into 2nd of 5 separate ch work 2tr, 2ch and 2tr, ss into 5th ch to form last tr.
Turn. 13[15] grs.
4th row 3ch, *2tr, 2ch and 2tr into next 2ch sp, rep from * to end, finishing with 1tr into 3rd of the 3ch. Turn.
Rep last row 3 times more. Fasten off.

Angel top left back yoke

Using No.3.50 (ISR) hook make 27[30] ch.
1st row Into 3rd ch from hook work 1dc, 1dc into each ch to end. Turn. 26[29] sts.
2nd row 3ch, miss first st, 1tr into each st to end. Turn.
3rd row 1ch, miss first st, 1dc into each st to end. Turn.
Rep 2nd and 3rd rows twice more, then work 2nd row again.
Shape shoulder
Next row Ss over first 4 sts, 1ch, 1dc into each st to end. Turn.
Next row 1ch, 1dc into each st to last 4[6] sts. Fasten off.

Angel top right back yoke

Work as given for left back yoke, reversing shoulder shaping.
Shape skirt
With RS of work facing, return to lower edge of left yoke and rejoin yarn.
1st row 3ch, into first st, 2tr, 1ch and 2tr into next st, *miss next 3 sts, 2tr, 1ch and 2tr into next st, rep from * to last 2[1] sts, 1tr into last st, 1tr into first st of right yoke,

miss, 2[0] sts, 2tr 1ch, 2tr into next st, *miss 3 sts, 2tr, 1ch and 2tr into next st, rep from * to last 2[3] sts, 1tr into last st. Turn.
2nd row 3ch, *2tr, 1ch and 2tr into next 1ch sp, rep from * to centre, 2tr, 1ch and 2tr into sp between 2 centre sts, *2tr, 1ch and 2tr into next 1ch sp, 1tr into 3rd of 3ch.
Turn. 13[15] grs.
3rd row As 3rd row of skirt front.
4th row As 4th row of skirt front.
Rep last row 3 times more. Fasten off.

To make up

Press under a damp cloth with a warm iron. Join shoulder and side seams. With RS of work facing and using No.3.50 (ISR) crochet hook, rejoin yarn to top of right back opening and work 1dc into each row end down side of opening, work buttonholes up other side of opening as foll: 2ch, 1dc into first and second tr row ends, 2ch, 2dc into next tr row, 2ch, 3dc, 2ch and 1dc into top of opening, cont round neck as foll: work 13dc evenly across left back neck to shoulder, 25dc all round front neck to next shoulder and 13dc across right back neck to top of opening. Turn. 51 sts.
Next row Work 1dc into each dc all round neck. Turn.
Next row 1ch to count as first dc, *miss 2 sts, 5tr into next st – called 1 shell –, miss 2 sts, 1dc into next st, rep from * all round. Fasten off.
Armhole edging Work 32dc evenly round each armhole, then work a round of shells, leaving only one dc between each shell and dc instead of two.
Sew on buttons to correspond with buttonholes.

Pants

Using No.3.50 (ISR) hook make 54[58] ch for front waist edge.
1st row Into 3rd ch from hook work 1dc, 1dc into each ch to end. 53[57] sts.
2nd row 3ch to count as first tr, miss first dc, 1tr into each st to end.
Turn.
3rd row 1ch to count as first dc, 1dc into each st to end.
Turn.
Rep 2nd and 3rd rows 2[3] times more, then work 2nd row again.
Shape legs
Next row Ss over first 4 sts, 1ch, 1dc into each st to last 4 sts, turn.
Next row Ss over first 4 sts, 3ch, 1tr into each st to last 4 sts, turn.
Next row Ss over first 3 sts, 1ch, 1dc into each st to last 3 sts, turn.
Next row Ss over first 2 sts, 3ch, 1tr into each st to last 2 sts, turn.
Next row Ss into first st, 1ch, 1dc into each st to last st, turn.
Next row Ss into first st, 3ch, 1tr into each

st to last st, turn.
Rep last 2 rows 2[3] times more. 15 sts.
Work 11 rows dc on these sts.

Shape back

Next row 3ch, 1tr into st at base of 3ch, 1tr into each st to last st, 2tr into last st. Turn.

Next row 1ch, 1dc into st at base of ch, 1dc into each st to last st, 2dc into last st. Turn.

Rep last 2 rows 3[4] times more. 31[35] sts.

Next row 3ch, 1tr into st at base of 3ch, 1tr into each st to last st, 2tr into last st. Turn.

Next row 1ch, 2dc into st at base of ch, 1dc into each st to last st, 3dc into last st. Turn.

Rep last 2 rows twice more. 49[53] sts.

Next row 3ch, 1tr into st at base of 3ch, 1tr into each st to last st, 2tr into last st. Turn.

Next row As 3rd row of pants.

Rep last 2 rows once more. 53[57] sts. Rep

2nd and 3rd rows of pants 4[5] times more. Fasten off.

To make up

Press as given for angel top. Join side seams.

Leg edging Work 1 round of dc round each leg, then work a round of shells as given for angel top, missing only one dc between each shell and dc instead of two.

Work herringbone casing over elastic on WS of waist.

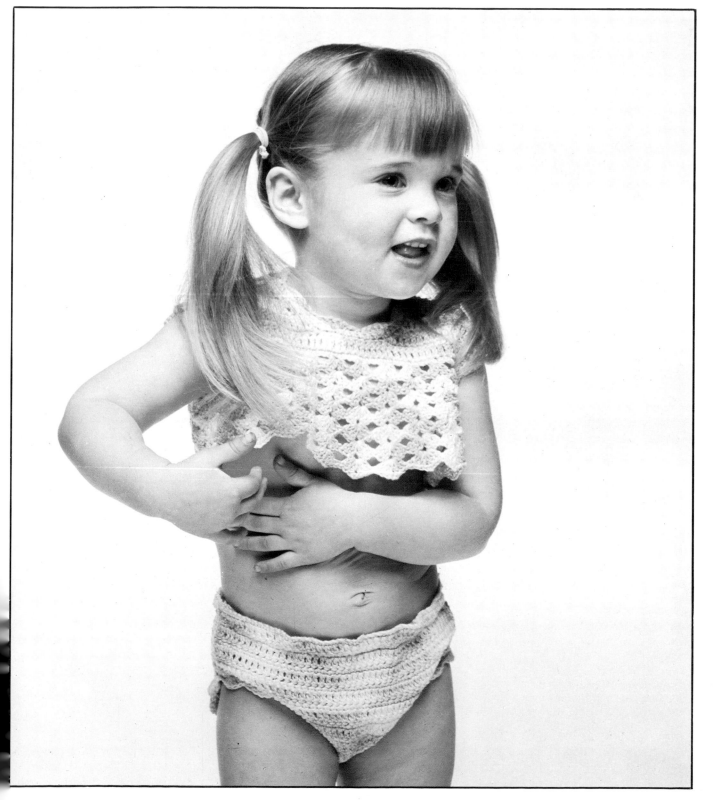

Delightful dress and matching head scarf

Sizes
To fit 51[56]cm (20[22]in) chest
Length to shoulder, 40[43]cm (15¾[17]in)
The figures in brackets [ ] refer to the 56cm (22in) size only

Tension
4 patts and 14 rows to 10cm (3.9in) over patt worked on No.3.00 (ISR) crochet hook

Materials
2[2] × 50grm balls Pingouin Superbebe or Age d'Or in main shade, A
2[2] balls of contrast colour, B
One No.3.00 (ISR) crochet hook
One button

Dress front
Using No.3.00 (ISR) hook and A, make 86[92]ch.
1st row Into 3rd ch from hook work 1dc, 1dc into each ch to end.
Turn. 85[91] sts.
2nd row (RS) 4ch, miss 3dc, *yrh, insert hook into next dc and draw through a loop, yrh and draw through first 2 loops on hook, (yrh, insert hook into same dc and draw through a loop, yrh and draw through first 2 loops on hook) twice, yrh and draw through all 4 loops on hook – called gr –, 3ch, miss 2dc, 1dc into next dc, 3ch, miss 2dc, rep from * to end, omitting 3ch, miss 2dc at end of last rep. Turn.
3rd row Working 3ch to count as first st work 1gr into first dc, *3ch, 1dc into next gr, 3ch, 1gr into next dc, rep from * ending with last gr into 2nd of 4ch.
Turn.
4th row Join in B. 4ch, *1gr into next dc, 3ch, 1dc into next gr, 3ch, rep from * omitting 3ch at end of last rep.
Turn.
5th row With B, as 3rd.
The last 2 rows form the patt. Cont in stripe sequence of 2 rows A and 2 rows B, rep them until 9[11] rows have been worked from beg.

Next row 4ch, 1gr into next dc, (3ch, 1dc into next gr, 3ch, 1gr into next dc) 3 times, *1ch, 1dc into next gr, 1ch, 1gr into next dc, *, (3ch, 1dc into next gr, 3ch, 1gr into next dc) 5[6] times, rep from * to * once more, patt to end.
Turn.
Next row Working 3ch to count as first st st work 1gr into first dc, (3ch, 1dc into next gr, 3ch, 1gr into next dc) 3 times, 3ch, 1dc into next gr, *1gr into next dc, 1dc into next gr, *, (3ch, 1gr into next dc, 3ch, 1dc into next gr) 5[6] times, rep from * to * once more, patt to end.
Turn.
Next row 4ch, (1gr into next dc, 3ch, 1dc into next gr, 3ch) 3 times, 1gr into gr at centre of dec, (3ch, 1dc into next gr, 3ch, 1g. into next dc) 4[5] times, 3ch, 1dc into next gr, 3ch, 1gr into gr at centre of dec, 3ch, 1dc into next gr, patt to end. Turn.
Next row Patt to end. Turn. 12[13] patts.
Patt 14 more rows, then rep the 4 dec rows, keeping the decs in line above previous ones. 10[11] patts. Cont without shaping until work measures 30[32]cm (11¾[12¾]in) from beg, ending with a WS row.
Shape armholes
Next row Miss first gr, dc and next gr, rejoin yarn to next dc, working 3ch to count as first st, work 1gr into same dc, patt to within 2nd dc from last, ending with 1gr into this dc. Turn. 7[8] patts.
Cont without shaping until armholes measure 7.5[8]cm (3[3¼]in) from beg, ending with a WS row.
Shape neck
Next row Working 3ch to count as first st work 1gr into first dc, 3ch, 1dc into next gr, 3ch, 1gr into next dc, 3ch, 1dc into next gr, turn.
Cont on these sts until armhole measures 10[11]cm (4[4¼]in) from beg, ending at armhole edge.
Shape shoulder
Next row Ss into first gr, 3ch, 1dc into next

dc, 3ch, 1htr into next gr.
Fasten off.
With RS of work facing, miss 3[4] gr in centre for front neck, rejoin yarn to next gr, 4ch, patt to end. Turn. Complete to match first side, reversing shaping.

Dress back
Work as given for front until armhole shaping has been completed. Cont without shaping until armholes measure 2[3]cm (¾[1¼]in) from beg, ending with a WS row. Mark centre st of work with a coloured thread.
Divide for opening
Next row Patt to marker, turn.
Cont on these sts until armhole measures same as front to shoulder, ending at armhole edge.
Shape shoulder
Next row Ss over first dc and gr, 3ch, 1dc into next dc, 3ch, 1dc into next gr, 3ch, 1gr into next dc.
Fasten off.
With RS of work facing, rejoin yarn to centre st, patt to end. Turn. Complete to match first side, reversing shaping.

To make up
Press each piece under a damp cloth with a warm iron. Join shoulder and side seams.
Neck edging Using No.3.00 (ISR) hook, A and with RS of work facing, work a row of dc round neck edge. Complete with a row in patt as 2nd row of front.
Complete armholes in same way. Sew button to top of back opening and make a loop on other side to correspond.

Headscarf
Using No.3.00 (ISR) hook and A, make 99ch.
1st row Join in B. Into 6th ch from hook work 1gr, 3ch, miss 2ch, 1dc into next ch, *3ch, miss 2ch, 1gr into next ch, 3ch, miss 2ch, 1dc into next ch, rep from * to end.
Turn. 16 patts.
2nd row As 3rd row of dress front.
3rd row With A, as 4th row of dress front.
4th row Ss to first gr, 4ch, 1gr into next dc, patt to end, finishing with 1dc into last gr, turn.
Cont in patt and stripe sequence of 2 rows B and 2 rows A throughout, dec ½ patt at each end of every foll alt row until 1 patt rem.
Fasten off.
Front edging
Using No.3.00 (ISR) hook, A and with RS of work facing, work 1 row of patt along front edge.

To make up
Press as given for dress. Cut rem yarn into lengths of approx 14cm (5½in) and knot a fringe along both shaped edges. Trim fringe.

Charming motif cushions

Sizes

Each cushion measures 40.5cm (*16in*) square

Tension

Brown and orange motif measures 7.5cm
(*3in*) square worked on No.2.00 (ISR)
crochet hook
Turquoise and lemon motif measures
11.5cm (*4½in*) between widest points
worked on No.2.00 (ISR) crochet hook

Materials

Both cushions 1 × 20grm ball Twilley's
Lyscordet in each of two colours, A and B
One No.2.00 (ISR) crochet hook
0.45 metres (*½ yard*) of 0.90 metre (*36in*) wide
gingham material
40.5cm (*16in*) square cushion pad

Brown and orange motifs
1st motif

Using No.2.00 (ISR) hook and A, make 8ch.
Join with a ss into first ch to form a circle.
1st round 4ch, leaving last loop of each on
hook work 2dtr into circle, yrh and draw
through all loops on hook – called 1st
cluster –, *4ch, leaving last loop of each on
hook work 3dtr into circle, yrh and draw
through all loops on hook – called 1 cluster –,
rep from * 6 times more, 4ch. Join with a ss
to top of 1st cluster. Break off A.
2nd round Join B with a ss into any 4ch
loop, work 1st cluster into this loop, (4ch
and 1 cluster) twice into same loop, *3ch,
1dc into next 4ch loop, 3ch, 1 cluster into
next 4ch loop, (4ch and 1 cluster) twice into
same loop, rep from * twice more, 3ch, 1dc
into next 4ch loop, 3ch. Join with a ss to
top of first cluster. Break off B.
3rd round Join A with a ss to next 4ch loop,
1dc into same loop, *9ch, 1dc into next 4ch
loop, (5ch, 1dc into next 3ch loop) twice,
5ch, 1dc into next 4ch loop, rep from * 3
times, omitting last dc. Join with a ss into
first dc.
4th round Using A work *7tr, 3ch and
7tr into 9ch loop, 1dc into next 5ch loop,
3dc, 3ch and 3dc into next 5ch loop, 1dc
into next 5ch loop, rep from * 3 times more,

Join with a ss into top of first tr. Fasten off.
2nd motif
Work as given for 1st motif until 3rd round
has been completed.
4th round Work 7tr into first 9ch loop,
2ch, ss into corresponding 5ch loop on 1st
motif, 2ch, 7tr into same 9ch loop on 2nd
motif, 1dc into next 5ch loop, 3dc into next
5ch loop, 1ch, ss into corresponding 3ch
loop on 1st motif, 1ch, 3dc into same 5ch
loop on 2nd motif, 1dc into next 5ch loop,
7tr into next 9ch loop, 2ch, ss into
corresponding 5ch loop on 1st motif, 2ch,
7tr into same 9ch loop on 2nd motif,
complete as given for 1st motif. Fasten off.
Make and join the 3rd and 4th motifs in the
same way so that they form a square.
5th motif
Work as given for 1st motif, using B
instead of A and A instead of B and
joining to one free side of 1st motif on 4th
round.
6th motif
Work as given for 5th motif and join on the
4th round to other free side of 1st motif,
also joining to 5th motif at one corner.
7th and 8th motifs
Work as given for 5th motif, but join to
the two free sides of 3rd motif and to each
other at one corner.

Small flowers

Using A only, work as given for 1st motif
until 1st round has been completed.
2nd round Work 3dc, 3ch and 3dc into
each 4ch loop to last loop, 3dc into last loop,
1ch, ss to free 5ch loop of motif of opposite
colour, 1ch, 3dc into same 4ch loop. Join
with a ss to first dc. Fasten off.
Make 3 more motifs in A and 2 in B.

To make up

Cut a piece of gingham 86.5cm (*34in*)
square, fold in half and seam along 3 edges,
leaving 1.5cm (*½in*) turnings. Turn to RS and
insert a piece of card into the case to make
pinning the motifs easier. Pin crochet in
position on cover, then sew using a
matching colour. Place pad in cover, turn in

raw edges and oversew the seam.

Turquoise and lemon motifs
1st motif

Using No.2.00 (ISR) hook and A, make
8ch. Join with a ss into first ch to form a
circle.
1st round 6ch to count as first tr and 3ch,
1tr into circle, *3ch, 1tr into circle, rep from
* 3 times more, 3ch. Join with a ss into 3rd
of 6ch.
2nd round *Into next 3ch loop work 1dc,
1htr, 3tr, 1htr and 1dc, rep from * all round.
3rd round 5ch, *working across back work
1dc round stem of next tr in 1st round, 5ch,
rep from * 4 times more. Join with a ss
round last stem, taking in first 5ch.
4th round *Into next 5ch loop work 1dc,

1htr, 5tr, 1htr and 1dc, rep from * to end.

5th round *7ch, 1dc into back of dc between petals of previous round, rep from * all round, ending with 7ch, 1dc into back of next dc between petals, taking in the base of the 7ch.

6th round Into next 7ch loop work 1dc, 1htr, 7tr, 1htr and 1dc, rep from * all round. Join with a ss into first dc. Break off A.

7th round Join in B to dc between petals, 1dc into same place, *8ch, 1dc into 4th of 7tr of next petal, 8ch, 1dc between petals, rep from * all round. Join with a ss into first dc.

8th round Ss into first 4ch, 1dc into 8ch loop, *12ch, 1dc into next 8ch loop, 1dc into next 8ch loop, rep from * omitting dc at end of last rep. Join with a ss into first dc.

9th round *1dc into each of next 6ch, 3ch, 1dc into each of next 6ch, 1dc between 2dc of previous round, rep from * to end. Join with a ss into first dc. Fasten off.

2nd motif
Work as given for 1st motif until 8th round has been completed.

9th round 1dc into each of first 6ch, 1ch, ss into 3ch loop on 1st motif, 1ch, 1dc into each of next 6ch on 2nd motif, work as given for 1st motif, joining as before on the next 3ch loop, complete as given for 1st motif. Fasten off.

Make 7 more motifs, joining as before into 3 rows with 3 motifs in each.

Small motif
Using No.2.00 (ISR) hook and A, make 5ch.

Join with a ss into first ch to form a circle.

1st round 3ch, 11tr into circle. Join with a ss into 3rd of 3ch.

2nd round 1dc into sp between 3ch and next tr, *8ch, miss next 2 sp between tr, 1dc into sp between next 2tr, rep from * to end. Join with a ss into same sp as first dc.

3rd round Ss into first 4ch, 1dc into 8ch loop, *6ch, 1dc into join of large motifs, 6ch, 1dc into next 8ch loop on small motif, rep from * 3 times more, working last dc into first dc.
Fasten off.
Make 3 more small motifs and join to large motifs in the same way.

To make up
Complete as given for other cushion.

41

Bonny baby bonnet

Sizes
Width round brim, 33[37]cm (13[14½]in)
The figures in brackets [ ] refer to the 37cm (14½in) size only

Tension
12dc and 11 rows to 5cm (2in) over patt worked on No.2.50 (ISR) crochet hook

Materials
3[3]×25grm balls Sirdar Snuggly Wash'n'Wear Baby 4 ply
One No.2.50[3.00] (ISR) crochet hook

Bonnet
Using No.2.50[3.00] (ISR) hook make 4ch. Join with a ss to first ch to form circle.

1st round 3ch to count as first tr, 11tr into circle. Join with a ss to 3rd of 3ch. 12tr.
2nd round 1ch to count as first dc, 1tr round first 3ch of previous round, *1dc into next tr, 1tr round bar of same tr – called raised tr –, rep from * to end. Join with a ss into first 1ch. 12 raised tr with 1dc between each.
3rd round 1ch, 1dc into next raised tr, 1 raised tr into same raised tr, *1dc into next dc, 1dc into next raised tr, 1 raised tr into same raised tr, rep from * to end. Join with a ss into first ch.
4th round 1ch, *1dc into each dc to next raised tr, 1 raised tr into next raised tr, rep from * to end. Join with a ss into first ch. Rep 4th round 3 times more. 6dc between each raised tr. 12 sections.
Next row 1ch, 1dc into each st over 11

sections, turn.
Next row 1ch, 1dc into each dc over 11 sections.
Turn.
Next row 3ch, *miss 1dc, 1tr into next dc, 1tr into missed dc – called crossed tr –, rep from * to last st, 1tr into last st. Turn.
Next row 1ch, 1dc into each tr to end, 1dc into turning ch. Turn.

Rep last 2 rows 8 times more.
Fasten off.

To make up
Fold last 4 rows of bonnet on to RS to form brim.
Lower edging Using No.2.50[3.00] (ISR) hook work 3 rows dc along lower edge, working through double thickness of brim.
Brim edging Rejoin yarn to first crossed tr row and using No.2.50[3.00] (ISR) hook, work *3ch, 1dc into first ch, 1dc into next st, rep from * to end.
Turn.
Next row Into dc row work *3ch, 1dc into first ch, miss 1dc, 1dc into next st, rep from * to end. Turn. Rep last 2 rows once more.
Fasten off.
Using No.2.50[3.00] (ISR) hook and yarn double, make 70ch on each side of bonnet for ties.
Sew in ends.

A simple table setting

Size
115.5cm (45in) square

Tension
One motif measures 9cm (3½in) square

Materials
19 × 20grm balls Coats Chain Mercer-Crochet Cotton No.20
One No.1.25 steel crochet hook

First motif
Using No.1.25 (ISR) hook make 8ch. Join with a ss into first ch to form a circle.

1st round 16dc into circle. Join with a ss into first dc.

2nd round 1dc into same place as ss, *3ch, miss next dc, 1dc into next dc, rep from * 6 times, 3ch. Join with a ss into first dc.

3rd round Ss into first 3ch sp, 4ch, leaving last loop of each on hook work 3tr into same sp, yrh and draw through all loops on hook, *6ch, work a 4tr tr cluster into next 3ch sp by leaving the last loop of each tr tr on hook, yrh and draw through all loops on hook – called 1cl –, rep from * 6 times, 6ch. Join with a ss into top of first cl.

4th round 6ch, 1tr into same place as ss, *7tr into next 6ch sp, (1tr, 3ch, 1tr) into top of next cl, rep from * 6 times, 7tr into next 6ch sp. Join with a ss into 3rd of first 6ch.

5th round *Into next 3ch sp work 2dc, 3ch, 2dc, miss next tr, 1dc into next tr, 1htr into next tr, 1tr into next tr, (2dtr, 3ch, 2dtr) into next tr, 1tr into next tr, 1htr into next tr, 1dc into next tr, miss next tr, rep from * 7 times. Join with a ss into first dc.

6th round Ss into first 3ch sp, 12ch, 1tr tr into same sp, 7ch, 1dc into next sp, 7ch, (1tr, 5ch, 1tr) into next sp, 7ch, 1dc into next sp, 7ch, *(1tr tr, 7ch, 1tr tr) into next sp, 7ch, 1dc into next sp, 7ch, (1tr, 5ch, 1tr) into next sp, 7ch, 1dc into next sp, 7ch, rep from * twice. Join with a ss into 5th of first 12ch.

7th round 1dc into 7ch sp just completed, (6tr, 3ch, 6tr) into next 7ch sp (i.e. between pair of tr tr of previous round), 1dc into next 7ch sp, 11ch, 1dc into next 7ch sp, 8tr into next 5ch sp, 1dc into next 7ch sp, 11ch, *1dc into next sp, (6tr, 3ch, 6tr) into next sp, 1dc into next sp, 11ch, 1dc into next sp, 8tr into next sp, 1dc into next sp, 11ch, rep from * twice. Join with a ss into first dc. Fasten off.

Second motif
Work as given for first motif for 6 rounds.

7th round 1dc into 7ch sp just completed, *6tr into next 7ch sp, 1ch, 1dc into corresponding sp on first motif, 1ch, 6tr into same sp on second motif, 1dc into next 7ch sp, *, 5ch, 1dc into next sp on first motif, 5ch, 1dc into next 7ch sp on second motif, 8tr into next 5ch sp, 1dc into next 7ch sp, 5ch, 1dc into next sp on first motif, 5ch, 1dc into next 7ch sp on second motif, rep from * to * once more, complete as given for first motif.

Make 13 rows of 13 motifs, joining each as second motif was joined to first. Where 4 corners meet, join third and fourth motifs to previous joining.

To make up
Darn in all ends. Press on wrong side under a damp cloth with a warm iron.

43

Traditional cover

Size

To fit single bed size
The figures in brackets [ ] refer to the double bed size

Tension

One complete patt measures 19cm ($7\frac{1}{2}$in)× 31.5cm ($12\frac{1}{2}$in) worked on No.3.50 (ISR) crochet hook

Materials

38[45]× 50grm balls Twilley's Stalite
One No.3.50 (ISR) crochet hook

1st strip

Using No.3.50 (ISR) hook make 80ch.
Base row Into 6th ch from hook work 1tr, *1ch, miss next ch, 1tr into next ch, rep from * to end. Turn. 38 ch sp.
Commence patt.

1st row 3ch to count as first tr, miss next tr, 1dtr into next tr, working behind dtr just made work 1dtr into missed tr – called cross 1 –, cross 1 over next 2tr and ch sp, 1tr into next tr, 1tr into next sp, 1tr into next tr, *1ch, 1tr into next tr, rep from * 25 times more, 1tr into next sp, 1tr into next tr, (cross 1) twice, 1tr into 4th of 5ch (end subsequent 1st patt rows with 1tr into 3rd of 3ch). Turn.

2nd row 3ch, (cross 1) twice working over previous crossed dtr, 1tr into each of next 3tr, 1tr into next sp, 1tr into next tr, *1ch, 1tr into next tr, rep from * 23 times more, 1tr into next sp, 1tr into each of next 3tr, (cross 1) twice, 1tr into 3rd of 3ch. Turn.

3rd row 3ch, (cross 1) twice, 1tr into each of next 5tr, 1tr into next sp, 1tr into next tr, *1ch, 1tr into next tr, rep from * 21 times more, 1tr into next sp, 1tr into each of next 5tr, (cross 1) twice, 1tr into 3rd of 3ch. Turn.

4th row 3ch, (cross 1) twice, 1tr into next tr, 1ch, miss 1tr, 1tr into each of next 5tr, 1tr into next sp, 1tr into next tr, (1ch, 1tr into next tr) 9 times, (1tr into next sp, 1 tr into next tr) twice, (1ch, 1tr into next tr) 9 times, 1tr into next sp, 1tr into each of next 5tr, 1ch, miss 1tr, 1tr into next tr, (cross 1) twice, 1tr into 3rd of 3ch. Turn.

5th row 3ch, (cross 1) twice, 1tr into next tr, 1ch, 1tr into next tr, 1ch, miss 1tr, 1tr into each of next 5tr, 1tr into next sp, 1tr into next tr, (1ch, 1tr into next tr) 7 times, 1tr into next sp, 1tr into each of next 5tr, 1tr into next sp, 1tr into next tr, (1ch, 1tr into next tr) 7 times, 1tr into next sp, 1tr into each of next 5tr, 1ch, miss 1tr, 1tr into next tr, 1ch, 1tr into next tr, (cross 1) twice, 1tr into 3rd of 3ch. Turn.

6th row 3ch, (cross 1) twice, 1tr into next tr, (1ch, 1tr into next tr) twice, 1ch, miss 1tr, 1tr into each of next 5tr, 1tr into next sp, 1tr into next tr, (1ch, 1tr into next tr) 5 times, 1tr into next sp, 1tr into each of next 9tr, 1tr into next sp, 1tr into next tr, (1ch, 1tr into next tr) 5 times, 1tr into next sp, 1tr into each of next 5tr, 1ch, miss 1tr, 1tr into next tr, (1ch, 1tr into next tr) twice, (cross 1) twice, 1tr into 3rd of 3ch. Turn.

7th row 3ch, (cross 1) twice, 1tr into next tr, (1ch, 1tr into next tr) 3 times, 1ch, miss 1tr, 1tr into each of next 5tr, 1tr into next sp, 1tr into next tr, (1ch, 1tr into next tr) 3 times, 1tr into next sp, 1tr into each of next 5tr, 2ch, 1dtr into next tr, miss 1tr, 1dtr into next tr, 2ch, 1tr into each of next 5tr, 1tr into next sp, 1tr into next tr, (1ch, 1tr into next tr) 3 times, 1tr into next sp, 1tr into each of next 5tr, miss 1tr, 1ch, 1tr into next tr, (1ch, 1tr into next tr) 3 times, (cross 1) twice, 1tr into 3rd of 3ch. Turn.

8th row 3ch, (cross 1) twice, 1tr into next tr, (1ch, 1tr into next tr) 4 times, 1ch, miss 1tr, 1tr into each of next 5tr, 1tr into next sp, 1tr into next tr, 1ch, 1tr into next tr, 1tr into next sp, 1tr into each of next 5tr, miss 2tr, 3ch, 1dc into top of 2ch from 7th row, 1dc into each of next 2dtr, 1dc into top of 2ch, 3ch, miss 2tr, 1tr into each of next 5tr, 1tr into next sp, 1tr into next tr, 1ch, 1tr into next tr, 1tr into next sp, 1tr into each of next 5tr, 1ch, miss 1tr, 1tr into next tr, (1ch, 1tr into next tr) 4 times, (cross 1) twice, 1tr into 3rd of 3ch. Turn.

9th row 3ch, (cross 1) twice, 1tr into next tr, (1ch, 1tr into next tr) 5 times, 1ch, miss 1tr, 1tr into each of next 5tr, 1tr into next sp, 1tr into each of next 5tr, miss 2tr, 5ch, 1dc into each of next 4dc, 5ch, miss 2tr, 1tr into each of next 5tr, 1tr into next sp, 1tr into each of next 5tr, 1ch, miss 1tr, 1tr into next tr, (1ch, 1tr into next tr) 5 times, (cross 1) twice, 1tr into 3rd of 3ch. Turn.

10th row 3ch, (cross 1) twice, 1tr into next tr, (1ch, 1tr into next tr) 6 times, 1ch, miss 1tr, 1tr into each of next 7tr, miss 2tr, 7ch, 1dc into each of next 4dc, 7ch, miss 2tr, 1tr into each of next 7tr, 1ch, miss 1tr, 1tr into next tr, (1ch, 1tr into next tr) 6 times, (cross 1) twice, 1tr into 3rd of 3ch. Turn.

11th row 3ch, (cross 1) twice, 1tr into next tr, (1ch, 1tr into next tr) 6 times, 1tr into next sp, 1tr into each of next 7tr, 1tr into each of next 2ch, 5ch, 1dc into each of next 4dc, 5ch, 1tr into each of last 2ch, 1tr into each of next 7tr, 1tr into next sp, 1tr into next tr, (1ch, 1tr into next tr) 6 times, (cross 1) twice, 1tr into 3rd of 3ch. Turn.

12th row 3ch, (cross 1) twice, 1tr into next tr, (1ch, 1tr into next tr) 5 times, 1tr into next sp, 1tr into each of next 5tr, 1ch, miss 1tr, 1tr into each of next 5tr, 1tr into each of next 2ch, 4ch, 1dc into each of next 4dc, 4ch, 1tr into each of last 2ch, 1tr into each of next 5tr, 1ch, miss 1tr, 1tr into each of next 5tr, 1tr into next sp, 1tr into next tr, (1ch, 1tr into next tr) 5 times, (cross 1) twice, 1tr into 3rd of 3ch. Turn.

13th row 3ch, (cross 1) twice, 1tr into next tr, (1ch, 1tr into next tr) 4 times, 1tr into next sp, 1tr into each of next 5tr, 1ch, miss 1tr, 1tr into next tr, 1ch, 1tr into next tr, 1ch, miss 1tr, 1tr into each of next 5tr, 1tr into each of next 2ch, 1dtr into 2nd of 4dc, 1ch, 1dtr into next dc, 1tr into last 2ch, 1tr into each of next 5tr, 1ch, miss 1tr, 1tr into next tr, 1ch, 1tr into next tr, 1ch, miss 1tr, 1tr into each of next 5tr, 1tr into next sp, 1tr into next tr, (1ch, 1tr into next tr) 4 times, (cross 1) twice, 1tr into 3rd of 3ch. Turn.

14th row 3ch, (cross 1) twice, 1tr into next tr, (1ch, 1tr into next tr) 3 times, 1tr into next sp, 1tr into each of next 5tr, 1ch, miss 1tr, 1tr into next tr, (1ch, 1tr into next tr) 3 times, 1ch, miss 1tr, 1tr into each of next 5tr, 1tr into next dtr, 1tr into ch sp, 1tr into next dtr, 1tr into each of next 5tr, 1ch, miss 1tr, 1tr into next tr, (1ch, 1tr into next tr) 3 times, 1ch, miss 1tr, 1tr into each of next 5tr, 1tr into next sp, 1tr into next tr, (1ch, 1tr into next tr) 3 times, (cross 1) twice, 1tr into 3rd of 3ch. Turn.

15th row 3ch, (cross 1) twice, 1tr into next tr, (1ch, 1tr into next tr) twice, 1tr into next sp, 1tr into each of next 5tr, 1ch, miss 1tr, 1tr into next tr, (1ch, 1tr into next tr) 5 times, 1ch, miss 1tr, 1tr into each of next 9tr, 1ch, miss 1tr, 1tr into next tr, (1ch, 1tr into next tr) 5 times, 1ch, miss 1tr, 1tr into each of next 5tr, 1tr into next sp, 1tr into next tr, (1ch, 1tr into next tr) twice, (cross 1) twice, 1tr into 3rd of 3ch. Turn.

16th row 3ch, (cross 1) twice, 1tr into next tr, 1ch, 1tr into next tr, 1tr into next sp, 1tr into each of next 5tr, 1ch, miss 1tr, 1tr into next tr, (1ch, 1tr into next tr) 7 times, 1ch, miss 1tr, 1tr into each of next 5tr, 1ch, miss 1tr, 1tr into next tr, (1ch, 1tr into next tr) 7 times, 1ch, miss 1tr, 1tr into each of next 5tr, 1tr into next sp, 1tr into next tr, 1ch, 1tr into next tr, (cross 1) twice, 1tr into 3rd of 3ch. Turn.

17th row 3ch, (cross 1) twice, 1tr into next tr, 1tr into next sp, 1tr into each of next 5tr, 1ch, miss 1tr, 1tr into next tr, (1ch, 1tr into next tr) 9 times, (1ch, miss 1tr, 1tr into next tr) twice, (1ch, 1tr into next tr) 9 times, 1ch, miss 1tr, 1tr into each of next 5tr, 1tr into next sp, 1tr into next tr, (cross 1) twice, 1tr into 3rd of 3ch. Turn.

18th row 3ch, (cross 1) twice, 1tr into each of next 5tr, 1ch, miss 1tr, 1tr into next tr, (1ch, 1tr into next tr) 22 times, 1ch, miss 1tr, 1tr into each of next 5tr, (cross 1) twice, 1tr into 3rd of 3ch. Turn.

These 18 rows form patt. Rep them 9 times more, noting that on subsequent 1st rows you should substitute 'tr' instead of 'sp'. Fasten off.

Make 4[5] more strips in the same way.

Triangles

Using No.3.50 (ISR) hook, make 38ch.

Base row Into 4th ch from hook work 1tr, 1tr into each ch to end. Turn. 36tr.

1st row Ss into 2nd tr, 3ch, yrh and insert into next tr, yrh and draw through a loop, yrh and draw through 2 loops on hook, yrh and insert into next tr, yrh and draw through a loop, yrh and draw through 2 loops, yrh and draw through rem 3 loops – called work 2tr tog –, 1tr into each tr, ending with 1tr into 3rd of 3ch. Turn.

2nd row 3ch to count as first tr, 1tr into each of next 4tr, *1ch, miss 1tr, 1tr into next tr, rep from * to end, omitting to work into 3rd of 3ch. Turn. 14 ch sp.

3rd row Ss into first sp and next tr, 3ch, miss next sp, 1tr into next tr, *1ch, 1tr into next tr, rep from * to last 4 sts, 1tr into each of next 3tr, 1tr into 3rd of 3ch. Turn. Two sp dec.

4th row 3ch, 1tr into each of next 4tr, *1ch, 1tr into next tr, rep from * to last sp, turn. One sp dec.

5th row 3ch, miss first sp, 1tr into next tr, *1ch, 1tr into next tr, rep from * to last 4 sts, 1tr into each of next 3tr, 1tr into 3rd of 3ch. Turn. One sp dec.

Rep 4th and 5th rows 4 times more, then work 4th row again. One sp rem.

Next row Ss into sp and next tr, 3ch, 1tr into each of next 3tr, 1tr into 3rd of 3ch. Turn.

Next row 3ch, miss next tr, work 3tr tog. Fasten off.

Make 30[32] triangles in all.

To make up

Place RS of two strips tog and, using No.3.50 (ISR) hook, cont along one long side working 2dc into each pair of row ends. Fasten off. Join other strips in the same way.

Triangular edging Allowing one triangle for every 18 rows of patt on long sides and 2 triangles for each panel on one short side, join shaped edge of triangles to main section as given for joining strips, but work 1dc into each pair of loops. Fasten off.

Top edge Using No.3.50 (ISR) hook work 2dc into each sp to end. Fasten off.

Lay out work on a large flat surface (e.g. a sheet) and pull to shape. Press under a damp cloth with a warm iron. Leave to dry.

Enchanting motif cape for a little girl

Hood Cape diagram:
Join
A to A
B to B

← neck edge →

Size
Length to shoulder, 53.5cm (*21in*)

Tension
1 motif measures 7cm×7cm (*2¾in × 2¾in*) worked on No.3.50 (ISR) crochet hook

Materials
2×25grm balls Sirdar Wash'n'Wear 4 ply in each of six colours, A, B, C, D, E and F
One No.3.50 (ISR) crochet hook

Motif
Using No.3.50 (ISR) hook and A, make 6ch. Join with a ss into first ch to form a circle.
1st round 3ch to count as first tr, 2tr into circle, (1ch, 3tr) 3 times into circle, 1ch. Join with a ss into 3rd of 3ch. Break off A.
2nd round Join in B to any 1ch sp, (3ch, 2tr, 1ch, 3tr) into same sp, (1ch, 3tr) twice into next 1ch sp, rep from * twice more, 1ch. Join with a ss into 3rd of 3ch. Break off B.
3rd round Join in C to any 1ch sp, (3ch, 2tr, 1ch, 3tr) into same sp, *1ch, 3tr into next 1ch sp, (1ch, 3tr) twice into next 1ch sp, rep from * twice more, 1ch, 3tr into next 1ch sp, 1ch. Join with a ss into 3rd of 3ch. Break off C.
4th round Join in A to any 1ch sp, (3ch, 2tr, 1ch, 3tr) into same sp, *1ch, 3tr into next 1ch sp, 1ch, 3tr into next 1ch sp, (1ch, 3tr, 1ch, 3tr) into next 1ch sp, rep from * twice more, 1ch, 3tr into next 1ch sp, 1ch, 3tr into next 1ch sp, 1ch. Join with a ss into 3rd of 3ch. Fasten off.
Make 79 more motifs in the same way using all the colours and making as great a variety of colour combinations as possible.

To make up
Darn in all ends. Using a flat seam, join 70 motifs as shown in diagram to form cape.
Neck edging Using No.3.50 (ISR) hook, light colour and working across neck edge, ss into corner sp of motif on right-hand edge of cape, 3ch, 1tr into same sp, *1ch, 2tr into next 1ch sp, rep from * across neck edge, working last 2tr into last corner sp on last motif. Turn.
Next row 3ch, *2tr into next 1ch sp, rep from * to end, 1tr into 3rd of 3ch. Turn.
Next row 3ch, *1tr into sp between 2tr gr of previous row, rep from * to end, 1tr into 3rd of 3ch. Turn.
Next row 3ch, 1tr into each tr to end, 1tr into 3rd of 3ch. Fasten off.
Join rem 10 motifs as shown in diagram to form hood.
Neck edging Using No.3.50 (ISR) hook and same colour as neck edging of cape, rejoin yarn to neck edge of hood at corner sp, 3ch, 2tr into same sp, *3tr into next 1ch sp, rep from * to end, working last 3tr into last corner sp. Fasten off.
Outer edging Using No.3.50 (ISR) hook and same colour as before, join yarn to any 1ch sp on outer edge and cont all round outer edge of cape and hood by working 3ch, 2tr into same sp, (1ch, 3tr) into each sp all round outer edge. Join with a ss to first ch. Rep last round twice more.
Fasten off.
Neck ties Using No.3.50 (ISR) hook and all colours tog, work a ch approx 63.5cm (*25in*) long, leaving about 7.5cm (*3in*) at each end for tassels. Thread through spaces at neck.

Unusual cafe curtains to enhance your home

Size
152.5cm (*60in*) wide × 86.5cm (*34in*) deep

Tension
13 sp and 16 rows to 15cm (*6in*) over filet patt worked on No.2.50 (ISR) crochet hook

Materials
9 × 50grm balls Coton du Pingouin
One No.2.50 (ISR) crochet hook

1st motif
Using No.2.50 (ISR) hook make 9ch. Join with a ss into first ch to form ring.
1st round *2ch, 5dtr into ring, 2ch, 1dc into ring, rep from * 3 times more. Do not join.
2nd round 9ch, *1dtr into 3rd dtr of 5dtr gr, 6ch to form corner sp, 1dtr into same dtr, 5ch, 1dtr into next dc, 5ch, rep from * twice more, 1dtr into 3rd dtr of 5dtr gr, 6ch, 1dtr into same dtr, 5ch. Join with a ss to 4th of 9ch.
3rd round 2dc into first ch sp, 5ch, ss into first ch – called 1 picot –, 2dc into same sp, *2dc into next ch sp, 1 picot, (2dc into same sp, 1 picot) twice, 2dc into same sp, (2 dc into next ch sp, 1 picot, 2dc into same sp) twice, rep from * twice more, 2dc into next ch sp, 1 picot, (2dc into same sp, 1 picot) twice, 2dc into same sp, 2dc into next ch sp,

1 picot, 2dc into same sp. Join with a ss to first dc.
4th round 9ch, 1dtr into first dc of corner sp, *5ch, 1dtr into centre picot of corner sp, 6ch, 1dtr into same picot, (5ch, 1dtr into first dc of next ch sp) 3 times, rep from * twice more, 5ch, 1dtr into centre picot of corner, 6ch, 1dtr into same picot, 5ch, 1dtr into first dc of next ch sp, 5ch. Join with a ss to 4th of 9ch.
5th round (2dc into next ch sp, 1 picot, 2dc into same sp) twice, *2dc into next ch sp, (1 picot, 2dc into same sp) 3 times, (2dc into next sp, 1 picot, 2dc into same sp) 4 times, rep from * twice more, 2dc into next sp, (1 picot, 2dc into same sp) 3 times, (2dc into next sp, 1 picot, 2dc into same sp) twice. Join with a ss to first dc.
6th round 9ch, (1tr into first dc of next ch sp, 6ch) twice, miss 1dc, 1 picot and 1dc, 1tr into next dc, *9ch, miss 1 picot and 1dc, 1tr into next dc, 6ch, 1tr into first dc of next ch sp, (6ch, 1tr into first dc of next ch sp) 4 times, 6ch, miss 1dc, 1 picot and 1dc, 1tr into next dc, rep from * twice, 9ch, miss 1 picot and 1dc, 1tr into next dc, (6ch, 1tr into first dc of next ch sp) twice, 6ch. Join with a ss to 3rd of 9ch. Fasten off.

2nd motif
Work as given for 1st motif until 5th round has been worked.
6th round 9ch, (1tr into first dc of next sp, 6ch) twice, miss 1dc, 1 picot and 1dc, 1tr into next dc, 5ch, ss into 5th of 9ch at corner of 1st motif, 5ch, miss 1 picot and 1dc on 2nd motif, 1tr into next dc, (3ch, ss into next ch loop of first motif, 3ch, 1tr into first dc of next ch sp on 2nd motif) 5 times, 3ch, ss into next ch loop of first motif, 3ch, miss 1dc, 1 picot and 1dc on 2nd motif, 1tr into next dc, 5ch, ss into 5th of 9ch at corner of 1st motif, 5ch, complete as given for 1st motif. Continue in this way until 11 motifs have been worked.

Main section
With RS of work facing, rejoin yarn to top right-hand corner of end motif at 5th of 9ch, 1dc into same ch, 4dc into next ch loop, 4dc into each ch loop to last 9ch loop, 1dc into 5th of 9ch. Turn. 346dc.
Next row 1ch to count as first dc, 1dc into each dc to end. Turn.
Rep last row once more.
Next row 5ch, miss next 2dc, *1tr into next dc, 2ch, miss 2dc, rep from * to end, 1tr into last dc. Turn. 115 sp.
Next row 5ch, 1tr into next tr, *2ch, 1tr into next tr, rep from * ending with last tr into 3rd of 5ch. Turn.
Rep last row 62 times or until curtain measures required length less 8cm (*3¼in*).
Divide for top
Next row Patt over first 3 sp, turn.

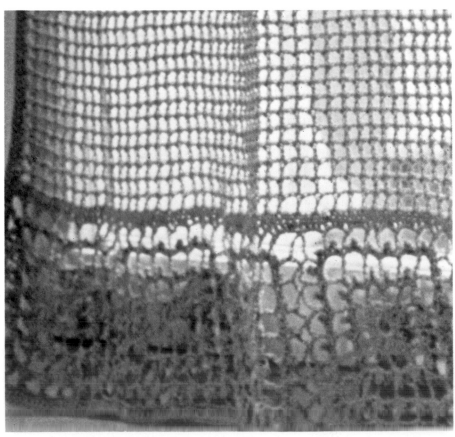

Work 15 rows in patt over these 5 sp. Fasten off.

Return to top of curtain, *miss next 4tr, rejoin yarn to next tr, 5ch to count as first tr and 2ch, patt over next 5 sp, turn and work 15 rows patt, rep from * until there are 12 tabs. Fasten off.

Edging

Rejoin yarn to lower edge of motifs and work 3 rows dc as given for motifs top. Do not turn at end of last row. Work 1 more dc into same place as last dc, cont up side of curtain, working 1dc into each dc row end, 3dc into each ch loop of motif, 1dc into each dc row end and 2dc into each row end up to corner sp of first tab, 6dc into corner sp of tab, 2dc into each sp to next corner, 6dc into corner sp, 2dc into each sp and 6dc into corner sp, 2dc into each sp and 6dc into

corner tabs until side edge of curtain is reached, complete to match first side. Turn.

Next row 1ch, 1dc into each dc and 2dc into corners all round. Turn.

Rep last row once more. Fasten off.

To make up

Press under a damp cloth with a warm iron. Fold tabs in half to WS and sl st down along top edge so forming loops for curtain rod.

Sunny-day shades

Size
61cm (*24in*) wide by 61cm (*24in*) long

Tension
38tr and 17 rows to 10cm (*3.9in*) over tr worked on No.1.75 (ISR) crochet hook

Materials
6×20grm balls Twilley's Twenty Crochet Cotton
One No.1.75 (ISR) crochet hook
Roller blind kit, 61cm (*24in*) wide

1st motif
Using No.1.75 (ISR) hook make 6ch. Join with a ss into first ch to form circle.
1st round 1ch to count as first dc, 11dc into circle. Join with a ss into first ch. 12dc.
2nd round 4ch, leaving last loop of each on hook work 2dtr into st at base of ch, yrh and draw through all loops on hook, *3ch, leaving last loop of each on hook work 3dtr into next dc, yrh and draw through all loops on hook, rep from * 10 times more, 3ch. Join with a ss into 4th of first 4ch.
3rd round Ss to centre of first 3ch loop, 1dc into same loop, *(5ch, 1dc into next 3ch loop) twice, 7ch, 1dc into next 3ch loop, rep from * 3 times more, omitting dc at end of last rep. Join with a ss into first dc. Fasten off.

2nd motif
1st to 2nd rounds Work as given for 1st motif.
3rd round Ss to centre of first 3ch loop, 1dc into same loop, (2ch, 1dc into corresponding 5ch loop on 1st motif, 2ch, 1dc into next 3ch loop on 2nd motif) twice, 3ch, 1dc into 4th of 7ch on 1st motif, 3ch, 1dc into next 3ch loop on 2nd motif, complete as given for 1st motif.
Work 12 more motifs in the same way, joining into a strip.

Main section
Rejoin yarn to 7ch sp at corner of first motif and cont along one long edge of motif strip, work 4dc into corner sp, 5dc into each of next two 5ch sp, 3dc into next corner sp, *3dc into next corner sp, 5dc into each of next two 5ch sp, 3dc into next corner sp, rep from * to end, working 4dc into last corner sp. Turn.

Next row 1ch, 1dc into each dc to end. Turn. 226dc.
Rep last row 8 times more.
Next row 4ch, miss first dc, *1tr into next dc, 1ch, miss next dc, rep from * to end, 1tr into last dc. Turn. 112 sp.
Next row 4ch, miss first tr, *1tr into next tr, 1ch, rep from * to end, 1tr into 3rd of first 4ch. Turn.
Rep last row 3 times more.
Next row 3ch, 1tr into first sp, *1tr into next tr, 1tr into next sp, rep from * to end, 1tr into 3rd of 4ch. Turn.
Next row 3ch, miss first tr, 1tr into each tr to end, finishing with 1tr into 3rd of 3ch. Turn.
Rep last row for the required length.
Fasten off.
Lower edging Rejoin yarn to corner sp on other long edge of motif strip, into 1st motif only work 3dc into corner sp, 5dc into each of next two 5ch sp, 3dc into corner sp. Turn. Cont in dc, dec one st at each end of every row until one st rem. Fasten off.
Rejoin yarn to each motif in turn and work a point on each in the same way.

To make up
Work one round dc all round outer edge, working 1dc, 5ch, 1dc into same place – called picot –, on each of the points at lower edge. Press under a damp cloth with a warm iron. Use a long herringbone stitch to enclose rigid bar to back of dc panel above the motif strip. Follow instructions given with kit to attach blind to roller.
Tassel Using No.1.75 (ISR) hook make 102ch. Into 3rd ch from hook work 1dc, 1dc into each ch to last ch, 3dc into last ch, then cont along other side of ch working 1dc into each ch to end. Fasten off.
Bobble Using No.1.75 (ISR) hook make 3ch. Join with a ss into first ch to form circle.
1st round 1ch, 7dc into circle. Do not join.
2nd round 2dc into each dc to end. 16dc. Do not join.
Working 1dc into each dc, work 7 continuous rounds on these 16dc. Work 2 sts tog all round. 8dc. Fasten off. Ease marble into cavity, run thread all round opening, pull up tightly and secure. Attach bobble to tassel and sew to rigid bar at back of blind.

Exotic counterpane

Size
To fit average single bed, 91.5cm (*36in*) wide

Tension
Motifs 1, 2 and 3 measure 21.5cm (*8½in*) square

Materials
Wendy Double Knitting
10 × 25grm balls in main shade, A
6 balls of contrast colour, B
7 balls of contrast colour, C
10 balls of contrast colour, D
11 balls of contrast colour, E
11 balls of contrast colour, F
7 balls of contrast colour, G
6 balls of contrast colour, H
6 balls of contrast colour, I
One No.5.50 (ISR) crochet hook

Counterpane
The counterpane is made of 8 square motifs using variations of 9 colours which are sewn tog and then borders and more motifs are worked on to the basic shape.

Square motif (1)
Using No.5.50 (ISR) hook and A, work 4ch. Join with a ss into first ch to form a circle.
1st round 3ch, 11tr into circle. Join with a ss into 3rd of 3ch.
2nd round Ss into first sp between tr, 3ch, 1tr into same sp, *2tr into next sp between tr, rep from * all round. Join with a ss into 3rd of 3ch. Break off A and join in B.
3rd round Ss into first sp between tr, 3ch, 2tr into same sp, miss next sp, *3tr into next sp, miss next sp, rep from * all round. Join with a ss into 3rd of 3ch. Break off B and join in G.
4th round Ss into first sp between grs of 3tr, (3ch, 2tr, 1ch – to form corner sp –, 3tr) into same sp, miss next 2 sp between tr, 1tr into each of next 4 sp, miss next 2 sp, *(3tr, 1ch, 3tr) into next sp, miss next 2 sp, 1tr into each of next 4 sp, miss next 2 sp, rep from * all round. Join with a ss into 3rd of 3 ch. Break off G and join in E.
5th round Ss into corner sp, (3ch, 2tr, 1ch, 3tr) into same sp, *miss next 2 sp between tr, 1tr into each of next 5 sp, miss next 2 sp, (3tr, 1ch, 3tr) into corner sp, rep from * all round. Join with a ss into 3rd of 3ch. Break

off E and join in A.
6th round Ss into corner sp, (3ch, 2tr, 1ch, 3tr) into same sp, *miss next 2 sp between tr, 1tr into each of next 6 sp, miss next 2 sp, (3tr, 1ch, 3tr) into corner sp, rep from * all round. Join with a ss into 3rd of 3ch. Break off A and join in G.
7th round Ss into corner sp, (3ch, 2tr, 1ch, 3tr) into same sp, *(miss next 2 sp between tr, 3tr into next sp – thus forming 1 shell) 3 times, (3tr, 1ch, 3tr) into corner sp, rep from * all round. Join with a ss into 3rd of 3ch. Fasten off G and join in C.
8th round Ss into corner sp, (3ch, 2tr, 1ch, 3tr) into same sp, *(miss next shell, 3tr into sp between next 2 shells) 4 times, miss next shell, (3tr, 1ch, 3tr) into corner sp, rep from * all round. Join with a ss into 3rd of 3ch. Break off C.
Make another motif in the same way.

Square motif (2)
Make 3 motifs in the same way as above, but work in colour sequence as foll:
1st and 2nd rounds Work with H.
3rd round Work with A.
4th round Work with D.
5th round Work with E.
6th round Work with B.
7th round Work with H.
8th round Work with C.

Square motif (3)
Make 3 motifs using colour sequence as foll:
1st and 2nd rounds Work with B.
3rd round Work with I.
4th round Work with B.
5th round Work with F.
6th round Work with G.
7th round Work with D.
8th round Work with C.
Using C, join these 8 motifs tog as shown in diagram.
Next round Join E to corner sp marked (a) on diagram, (3ch, 2tr, 1ch, 3tr) into corner, *work a 4tr shell into each sp between shells to (b) on diagram, 2tr into (b), (4tr shell into each sp to next corner, (3tr, 1ch, 3tr) into corner) twice, rep from * all round motif. Join with a ss into 3rd of 3ch. Break off E and join in D.
Next round Ss into corner sp, (3ch, 2tr,

1ch, 3tr) into same sp, *4tr shell into each
sp between shells to within one sp of point
(b), 1tr into next sp, miss 2tr at (b), 1tr into
next sp, (4tr shell into each sp to corner,
(3tr, 1ch, 3tr) into corner) twice, rep from *
all round. Join with a ss into 3rd of 3ch.
Break off D.

Semi-circular motif (4)
Using No.5.50 (ISR) hook and A, work 4ch.
Join with a ss into first ch to form a circle.
1st row 3ch, 6tr into circle. Turn.
2nd row Ss into first sp, 3ch, 1tr into same
sp, 2tr into each sp to end. Turn. Break off A
and join in B.
3rd row As 2nd row. Break off B and join
in E.
4th row Ss into first sp, 3ch, 1tr into same
sp, miss next sp, *3tr shell into next sp, miss
next sp, rep from * to last sp, 2tr into last sp.
Turn. Break off E and join in H.
5th row 3ch, 3tr shell into each sp between
shells, 1tr into 3rd of 3ch. Turn.
6th row Ss into first sp, 3ch, 1tr into same
sp, *4tr shell into next sp between shells,
rep from * to last sp, 2tr into last sp. Turn.
Break off H and join in E.
7th row 3ch, 4tr shell into first sp between
shells, *5tr shell into next sp, rep from * to
last sp, 4tr into last sp, 1tr into 3rd of 3ch.
Turn. Break off E.
Make 3 more motifs in the same way and
join to the main section as shown in the
diagram. Cont working a border round the
main shape as foll:
1st round With RS of work facing, join A
to point (*) on diagram and work 4tr shells
into each sp between shells to point (b), dec
at (b) by working 1tr into sp at either side of
previous dec, cont in shells to next corner,
4tr into corner, *3tr shell into 3rd tr of
previous 5tr shell, 3tr shell into next sp
between shells, rep from * all round
semi-circular motif and cont round shape
dec at each point (b), working (3tr, 1ch, 3tr)
into each corner and working round motifs
as shown above. Break off A and join in G.
2nd round As 1st round, but work 3tr
shells into each sp between shells round
motif 4. Break off G and join in F.
3rd round As 2nd round. Break off F and
join in G.
4th round Work all round 1tr into each tr
and 1tr into each sp, 1tr into each of 3 sp at
point (b), (3tr, 1ch, 3tr) into each corner,
missing 3tr between and after each corner
sp. Break off G and join in F.
5th round Work all round 1tr into each tr,
(3tr, 1ch, 3tr) into each corner and at point
(b) dec over 3tr by working 1tr into each of
the 3tr and leaving last loop of each on hook,
yrh and draw through all 4 loops on hook.
Break off F and join in D.
6th round As 4th round, but dec over 5tr at
each point (b). Break off D and join in F.

53

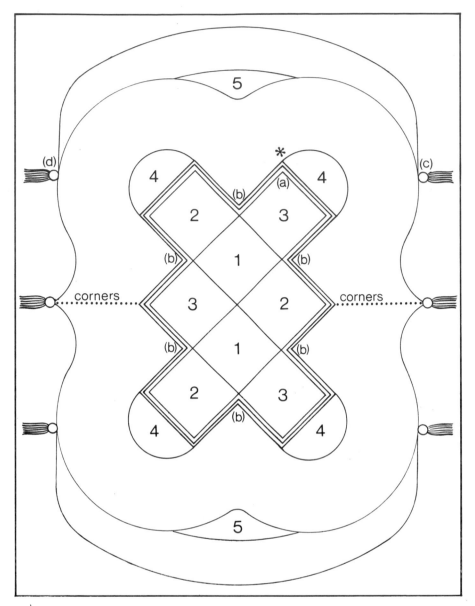

The following labels appear in the diagram:

5

(d)   (c)

4   (b)   (a)   4

2   3

(b)   *   (b)

1

(b)   (b)

corners   3   2   corners

(b)   (b)

1

(b)   (b)

2   3

4   (b)   4

5

2 sp, 1dtr between last 2 tr, 1dtr into 4th of 4ch. Turn.

10th row 4ch, 2dtr into first sp, 5dtr into next sp, *5tr into next sp, rep from * to last 2 sp, 5dtr into next sp, 2dtr into last sp, 1dtr into 4th of 4ch. Turn. Break off E and join in H.

11th row 4ch, 5dtr into first sp, * 5tr into next sp, rep from * to last sp, 5dtr into last sp, 1dtr into 4th of 4ch. Break off H. Make one more motif in the same way and join to the main section as shown in the diagram. Cont with border as foll:

15th round Join in A and work 1tr into each tr all round and (3tr, 1ch, 3tr) into 3rd tr of every 5tr shell. Break off A and join in D.

16th round *3tr shell into next sp, miss next 2 sp, rep from * all round, but work (3tr, 1ch, 3tr) into each corner. Break off D and join in A.

17th round Work 3tr shells into each sp and over motif(5), 4tr shells over the curves and (3tr, 1ch, 3tr) into each corner. Break off A and join in F.

18th round As 17th round. Break off F and join in C.

19th round As 17th round. Break off C and join in I.

20th round As 17th round. Break off I. Complete the counterpane by working the foll extensions:

1st row Join I to point marked (c) on diagram, 3ch and 3tr into same sp, 4tr shell into each sp between shells to point marked (d) on diagram. Turn. Break off I and join in B.

2nd row Ss into first sp between shells, 3ch and 3tr into same sp, 4tr shell into each sp to end. Turn. Break off B and join in E.

3rd row As 2nd row. Break off E and join in H.

4th row As 2nd row. Break off H and join in D.

5th row As 2nd row. Break off D and join in A.

6th row As 2nd row. Break off A. Work a similar extension at the opposite end of the cover, then work around the cover as foll:

Join E to any sp between shells, 3ch and 3tr into same sp, 4tr shell into each sp between shells all round, ss into 3rd of the 3ch. Break off E. Finish off all ends.

7th round As 5th round, but dec over 5tr at each point (b). Break off F and join in C.

8th round As 7th round, but work 2tr into every 10th tr round motif 4. Break off C and join in D.

9th round As 7th round. Break off D and join in F.

10th round As 7th round, but at each point (b) dec over 2tr, 1dtr into next tr, dec over next 2tr. Break off F and join in G.

11th round As 7th round, but dec over 2tr only at each point (b). Break off G and join in H.

12th round As 7th round, but do not dec at point (b) and work 5tr shells into each corner sp. Break off H and join in B.

13th round As 12th round, but work 5tr into 3rd tr of previous 5tr shell at corners. Break off B and join in E.

14th round As 12th round.

Motif(5)

Work as given for semi-circular motif(4) until 2nd row has been completed. Break off

A and join in B.

3rd row 3ch, miss first sp, 1tr into next sp, 1tr into each sp to last 2 sp, 1tr into each of last 2 sp. Turn. Break off B and join in E.

4th row 3ch, 1tr into first sp, *miss next sp, 3tr into next sp, miss next sp, 2tr into next sp, rep from * to end. Turn. Break off E and join in H.

5th row 3ch, *2tr into next sp, 3tr into next sp, rep from * to end, 1tr into 3rd of 3ch. Turn.

6th row 3ch, 1tr into first sp, *3tr into next sp, 2tr into next sp, rep from * to end. Turn. Break off H and join in E.

7th row 3ch, 3tr into each sp to end, 1tr into 3rd of 3ch. Turn. Break off E and join in H.

8th row 3ch, 2tr into first sp, *3tr into next sp, rep from * to last sp, 2tr into last sp, 1tr into 3rd of 3ch. Turn. Break off H and join in E.

9th row 4ch, 1dtr between 1st and 2nd tr, (4dtr into next sp) twice, * 4tr into next sp, rep from * to last 2 sp, 4dtr into each of next

To make up

Tassels (make 6) Cut 51cm (20in) lengths of every colour. Using 40 strands tog, tie them in the middle, fold in half and tie again 5cm (2in) from the top. Attach the tassels as shown in the diagram.

Fringe Cut lengths of every colour as given for tassels. Using 8 strands draw centre of threads through each sp between shells round edge and knot.

Table-mats to make for everybody

Size
20.5cm (*8in*) square

Tension
20 sts and 8 rows to 10cm (*3.9in*) over tr worked on No.4.00 (ISR) crochet hook

Materials
2 balls of cotton twine
One No.4.00 (ISR) crochet hook

Mat
Using No.4.00 (ISR) hook make 8ch. Join with a ss to first ch to form circle.

1st round 3ch to count as first tr, work 23tr into circle. Join with a ss to 3rd of first 3ch. 24tr.

2nd round 5ch, 3tr into first tr, * 3 ch, miss 4tr, 3tr into next tr, 2ch, 3tr into next tr, rep from * twice more, 3ch, miss 4tr, 2tr into ss of previous round. Join with a ss to 3rd of first 5ch.

3rd round Ss into first 2ch sp, 5ch, 3tr into same 2ch sp, *3ch, 1dc into next 3ch sp, 3ch, (3tr, 2ch, 3tr – called corner gr) into next 2ch sp, rep from * twice more, 3ch, 1dc into next 3ch sp, 3ch, 2tr into ss at beg of round. Join with a ss to 3rd of first 5ch.

4th round Ss into first 2ch sp, 5ch, 3tr into same 2ch sp, *3ch, 1dc into next 3ch sp, 5tr into next dc – called 1 shell –, 1dc into next 3ch sp, 3ch, corner gr into next 2ch sp, rep from * twice more, 3ch, 1dc into next 3ch sp, 1 shell into next dc, 1dc into next 3ch sp, 3ch, 2tr into ss at beg of round. Join with a ss to 3rd of first 5ch.

5th round Ss into first 2ch sp, 5ch, 3tr into same 2ch sp, *3ch, 1dc into next 3ch sp, 1 shell into next dc, 1dc into centre tr of next shell, 1 shell into next dc, 1dc into next 3ch sp, 3ch, corner gr into next 2ch sp, rep from * twice more, 3ch, 1dc into next 3ch sp, 1 shell into next dc, 1dc into centre tr of next shell, 1 shell into next dc, 1dc into next 3ch sp, 3ch, 2tr into ss at beg of round. Join with a ss to 3rd of first 5ch.

6th round Ss into first 2ch sp, 5ch, 3tr into same 2ch sp, *3ch, 1dc into next 3ch sp, (1 shell into next dc, 1dc into centre tr of next shell) twice, 1 shell into next dc, 1dc into next 3ch sp, 3ch, corner gr into next 2ch sp, rep from * twice more, 3ch, 1dc into next 3ch sp, (1 shell into next dc, 1dc into centre tr of next shell) twice, 1 shell into next dc, 1dc into next 3ch sp, 3ch, 2tr into ss at beg of round. Join with a ss to 3rd of first 5ch.

7th round As 6th, but working 4 shells on each side instead of 3.

8th round As 6th, but working 5 shells on each side. | Fasten off.

To make up
Darn in ends by separating strands and darning in each strand individually. Press under a damp cloth with a hot iron.

Table mats and coasters

Sizes
Table mat measures 34.5cm ($13\frac{1}{2}in$)×23cm ($9in$)
Coaster measures 14cm ($5\frac{1}{2}in$)×14cm ($5\frac{1}{2}in$)

Tension
28dc and 32 rows to 10cm ($3.9in$) over dc worked on No.2.00 (ISR) crochet hook; each motif measures 10cm ($4in$) square

Materials
15 balls Twilley's Lysbet for the complete set of six mats and six coasters
One No.2.00 (ISR) crochet hook

Table mat plain motif
Using No.2.00 (ISR) hook make 29ch.
1st row Into 3rd ch from hook work 1dc, 1dc into each ch to end. Turn. 28dc.
2nd row 1ch to count as first dc, miss first dc, 1dc into each dc, ending with last dc into turning ch. Turn.
Rep last row 30 times more. Fasten off.
Make 18 plain motifs in all for the complete set of table mats.

Table mat openwork motif
Using No.2.00 (ISR) hook make 6ch. Join with a ss into first ch to form circle.
1st round 5ch, *1tr into circle, 2ch, rep from * 6 times more. Join with a ss into 3rd of 5ch.
2nd round 3ch, 3tr into next 2ch sp, *1tr into next tr, 3tr into next 2ch sp, rep from * 6 times more. Join with a ss into 3rd of 3ch.
3rd round 6ch, miss 3tr, 1dc into next tr, 5ch, miss 3tr, *1dc into next tr, 5ch, miss 3tr, rep from * 5 times more. Join with a ss into first ch.
4th round Into each 5ch sp all round work 1dc, 1htr, 5tr, 1htr and 1dc.
5th round Ss into each of next 5 sts, 4ch to count as first dtr, leaving the last loop of each on hook work 2dtr into same place as last ss, yrh and draw through all loops on hook – called 3dtr cluster –, (3ch, 3dtr cluster) twice into same place as last cluster, *4ch, (1tr, 3ch and 1tr) into 3rd of next 5tr gr, 4ch, into 3rd of next 5tr gr work 3dtr cluster and (3ch, 3dtr cluster) twice, rep from * omitting three 3dtr clusters at end of last rep. Join with a ss into top of first cluster.
6th round Ss into next 3ch sp, 4ch, leaving the last loop of each on hook work 2dtr

into same sp, yrh and draw through all loops on hook, 3ch, 3dtr cluster into same sp, *7ch, into next 3ch sp work 3dtr cluster, 3ch and 3dtr cluster, 5ch, into next 3ch sp work 3dtr cluster, 3ch, 3dtr cluster, 5ch, 3dtr cluster into next 3ch sp, rep from * omitting 1 cluster, 3ch and 1 cluster at end of last rep. Join with a ss into top of first cluster.
7th round *3dc into next 3ch sp, 10dc into next 7ch sp, 3dc into next 3ch sp, 6dc into next 5ch sp, 3dc into next 3ch sp, 6dc into next 5ch sp, rep from * all round. Join with a ss into first dc. Fasten off.
Make 18 motifs in all for the complete set of table mats.

To make up
For each table mat take three openwork and three plain motifs. Using a flat seam join into two strips, one consisting of one plain motif in the centre of two openwork motifs and the other consisting of one openwork motif in the centre of two plain motifs. Sew the two strips together so that the alternating pattern is retained, and the mat consists of three motifs wide by two motifs deep.
Edging With RS of work facing, rejoin yarn to top right-hand corner of openwork motif on short side and using No.2.00 (ISR) hook, cont as foll:
1st round 28dc along edge of each motif to corner, 1ch for corner, 28dc along edge of each of motif to next corner, 1ch, 28dc along edge of each motif to next corner, 1ch, 28dc along edge of each motif to next corner, 1ch. Join with a ss into first dc. 280dc.
2nd round 5ch, miss 2dc, 1dc into next dc, *(5ch, miss 3dc, 1dc into next dc, rep from * to corner ch, 5ch, 1dc into corner ch) 4 times.
3rd round Into each 5ch sp all round work 1dc, 1htr, 3tr, 1htr and 1dc. Join with a ss into first dc. Fasten off.
Press under a damp cloth with a warm iron.

Coasters
Work as given for table mat openwork motif.
Edging Work as given for table mat edging, noting that on 1st round each dc will be worked into 1dc of last round of coaster.

A gracious lacy tablecloth

Size
Tablecloth measures 178cm (*70in*) in diameter

Tension
First motif measures 7cm (*2¾in*) diagonally from corner to corner when worked on No.1.50 (ISR) crochet hook

Materials
30 × 20grm balls Coats Chain Mercer-Crochet Cotton No.10
One No.1.50 (ISR) crochet hook
One No.1.75 (ISR) crochet hook
1.30 metres (*1⅜ yards*) of fabric, 122cm (*48in*) wide

Outer crochet section
First row, first motif
Using No.1.50 (ISR) hook make 24ch. Join with a ss into first ch to form circle.
1st round 3ch to count as first tr, 4tr into same place as ss, *1tr into each of next 5ch, 5tr into next ch, rep from * omitting 5tr at end of last rep. Join with a ss into 3rd of 3ch.
2nd round Ss into each of next 2tr, *3ch, 1dtr into same place as last ss, 3ch, leaving last loop of each on hook work 2dtr into same place as last dtr, yrh and draw through all loops on hook – called joint dtr –, 4ch, into same place as last st work (joint dtr, 3ch and joint dtr), 4ch, miss 4tr, 1dc into next tr, 4ch, miss 4tr, join dtr into next tr, rep from * omitting join dtr at end of last rep.
Join with a ss into first dtr.
3rd round *Into next ch loop work 2dc, 3ch and 2dc, into next ch loop work 3dc, 3ch and 3dc, into next ch loop work 2dc, 3ch and 2dc, 1dc into next loop, 5ch, 1dc into next loop, rep from * to end. Join with a ss into first dc. Fasten off.
Second motif
Work as given for first motif until 2nd round has been completed.
3rd round *Into next ch loop work 2dc, 3ch and 2dc, into next ch loop work 3dc, 1ch, ss into corresponding 3ch loop on first

motif, 1ch, 3dc into same loop on second motif, complete as given for previous motif. Make 62 more motifs, joining each as second motif was joined to first at opposite corner to previous join and joining last motif to first to correspond.
Second row, first motif
Using No.1.50 (ISR) hook make 32ch. Join with a ss into first ch to form circle.
1st round 3ch, 4tr into same place as ss, *1tr into each of next 7ch, 5tr into next ch, rep from * omitting 5tr at end of last rep. Join with a ss into 3rd of 3ch.
2nd round Ss into each of next 2tr, 3ch, 1dtr into same place as last ss, *3ch, into same place as last st work joint dtr, 5ch,

joint dtr, 3ch and a joint dtr, 5ch, miss 5tr, 1dc into next tr, 5ch, miss 5tr, joint dtr into next tr, rep from * omitting joint dtr at end of last rep. Join with a ss into first dtr.

3rd round Into next ch loop work 2dc, 3ch and 2dc, 3dc into next loop, 1ch, ss into centre 3ch loop at corner of any motif on previous row, 1ch, 3dc into same loop on 2nd round, into next loop work 2dc, 3ch and 2dc, 1dc into next loop, 7ch, 1dc into next loop, cont as given for 3rd round of first motif, working 7ch loop on each side instead of 5.

Second motif

Work as given for first motif until 2nd round has been completed.

3rd round Into next ch loop work 2dc, 3ch and 2dc, 3dc into next loop, 1ch, ss into next corner 3ch loop on next motif of previous row, cont as given for previous motif to within 3ch loop at next corner, 3dc into next loop, 1ch, ss into corresponding 3ch loop on previous motif, 1ch, 3dc into same loop on second motif, complete as given for previous motif.

Make 62 more motifs, joining each as second motif was joined to first and joining last motif to correspond.

Third row, first motif

Work as given for first motif on second row until 1st round has been completed.

2nd round As 2nd round of first motif on second row, working 7ch loop at each corner instead of 5.

3rd round As 3rd round of first motif on second row.

Second motif

Work as given for second motif on second row, working 7ch loop at each corner instead of 5 on 2nd round.

Make 62 more motifs, joining each as second motif was joined to first and joining last motif to first motif to correspond.

Fourth row

Using No.1.75 (ISR) hook, work as given for previous row.

First row of fillings

Using No.1.50 (ISR) hook make 14ch. Join with a ss into first ch to form circle.

1st round 3ch, 31tr into circle. Join with a ss into 3rd of 3ch.

2nd round 1dc into same place as ss, 7ch, ss into any join between motifs on first row, 7ch, ss into last dc worked, (1dc into each of next 2 sts on filling, 3ch, ss into next loop on motif, 3ch, ss into last dc made) 3 times, 1dc into each of next 2 sts on filling, 8ch, ss into next join between motifs, 8ch, ss into last dc made, *(1dc into each of next 2 sts on filling, 4ch, ss into next loop on motif, 4ch, ss into last dc made) 3 times, 1dc into each of next 2 sts on filling, *, 9ch, ss into next join between motifs, 9ch, ss into last dc made, rep from * to * once, 8ch, ss into next join between motifs, 8ch, ss into last dc made, (1dc into each of next 2 sts on filling, 3ch, ss into next loop on motif, 3ch, ss into last dc made) 3 times, 1dc into next dc. Join with a ss into first dc. Fasten off. Fill in all spaces between first and second rows in the same way.

Second row of fillings

Using No.1.50 (ISR) hook make 14ch. Join with a ss into first ch to form circle.

1st round 4ch, 31dtr into circle. Join with a ss into 4th of 4ch.

2nd round As 2nd round of previous filling, joining loops to second and third rows of motifs.

Fill in all spaces between second and third rows in the same way.

Third row of fillings

Using No.1.75 (ISR) hook work as given for second row of fillings, joining loops to third and fourth rows of motif.

Inner section
First row

Work as given for first row of outer section, having 20 motifs.

Second row

Work as given for third row of outer section, joining to previous row to correspond.

Filling

Work as given for first row of fillings, joining loops to correspond.

Centre

Using No.1.50 (ISR) hook make 20ch. Join with a ss into first ch to form circle.

1st round 4ch, 39dtr into circle. Join with a ss into 4th of 4ch.

2nd round 1dc into same place as ss, *25ch, ss into last dc made, 1dc into each of next 2dtr, rep from * omitting 1dc at end of last rep. Join with a ss into first dc. Fasten off.

3rd round Rejoin yarn to any 25ch loop, 1dc into same loop, *25ch, 1dc into next loop, rep from * ending with 25ch. Join with a ss into first dc.

4th round *Miss next ch, 1htr into next ch, 1tr into each of next 10ch, into next ch work 1tr, 3ch and 1tr, 1tr into each of next 10ch, 1htr into next ch, ss into next dc, rep from * ending with ss into first ss. Fasten off.

5th round Rejoin yarn to any 3ch loop, 1dc into same loop, *27ch, 3dc into next loop, rep from * ending with 27ch, 2dc into first loop. Join with a ss into first dc.

6th round Ss into next ch, 3ch, 1tr into each of next 13ch, 3dc into centre 3ch loop at corner of any motif on first row of inner section, *1tr into same ch on centre, 1tr into each of next 12ch, leaving last loop of each on hook work 1tr into each of next 2ch, yrh and draw through all loops on hook – called joint tr –, 1tr into each of next 13ch, 3dc into centre 3ch loop on next motif, rep from * ending with 1tr into same ch on centre, 1tr into each of next 12ch, leaving the last loop on hook work 1tr into next ch, insert hook into 3rd of 3ch, yrh and draw through all loops on hook. Fasten off.

To make up

Dampen crochet and pin out to measurements. Cut a circle of cloth, 119.5cm (*47in*) in diameter and from the centre of this circle cut another circle 53.5cm (*21in*) in diameter. Baste and stitch 0.5cm (*¼in*) hems on outer and inner edges of circle. Sew crochet in position as shown in photograph.

Circular table-cloth in contrasting shades of pink

Size
152.5cm (*60in*) diameter

Tension
20 sts and 10 rows to 10cm (*3.9in*) over tr worked on No.3.00 (ISR) crochet hook

Materials
2 × 50grm balls Twilley's Crysette in main shade, A
4 balls of contrast colour, B
7 balls of contrast colour, C

17 balls of contrast colour, D
One No.3.00 (ISR) crochet hook

Tablecloth
Using No.3.00 (ISR) hook and A, make 8ch. Join with a ss to first ch to form circle.

1st round 3ch to count as first tr, 23tr into circle. Join with a ss to 3rd of 3ch. 24 sts.

2nd round 4ch to count as first tr and 1ch, *1tr into next tr, 1ch, rep from * to end. Join with a ss to 3rd of 4ch.

3rd round 5ch to count as first tr and 2ch, *1tr into next tr, 2ch, rep from * to end. Join with a ss to 3rd of 5ch.

4th round Ss into first 2ch sp, 3ch, *1dc into next 2ch sp, 2ch, rep from * all round. Join with a ss into 2nd of 3ch.

5th round Ss into first ch sp, 4ch, *1dc into next ch sp, 3ch, rep from * all round. Join with a ss to 2nd of 3ch.

6th-8th rounds As 5th.

9th round Ss into first ch sp, 3ch, 1tr, 1ch, 2tr into same ch sp, *2tr, 1ch, 2tr into next 3ch sp, rep from * all round. Join with a ss to 3rd of 3ch.

10th round Ss into first ch sp, 3ch, 1tr into same ch sp, *2tr into sp between blocks of tr, 2tr into ch sp, rep from * all round, omitting last 2tr into ch sp. Join with a ss to 3rd of 3ch.

11th round Ss into sp between 2tr blocks, 3ch, 1tr into same sp, *2tr into next sp between 2tr blocks, rep from * all round. Join with a ss to 3rd of 3ch.

12th round Ss into sp between 2tr blocks, 3ch, 1tr into same sp, 1ch, *2tr into next sp between 2tr blocks, 1ch, rep from * all round. Join with a ss to 3rd of 3ch.

13th round As 12th.

14th round Ss into first ch sp, 3ch, 1tr, 1ch, 2tr into same ch sp, 2tr into next ch sp,

*(2tr, 1ch, 2tr) into next sp, 2tr into next sp, rep from * all round. Join with a ss to 3rd of 3ch. Fasten off A.
Join in B to any sp.

15th round 3ch, 1tr into same sp, miss 2tr, *2tr into next sp, miss 2tr, rep from * all round. Join with a ss to 3rd of 3ch.

16th round Ss into first sp between 2tr blocks, 3ch, 1tr into same sp, *2tr into next sp, rep from * all round. Join with a ss into 3rd of 3ch.

17th round Ss into first sp, 3ch, 1tr into same sp, 1ch, *2tr into next sp, 1ch, rep from * all round. Join with a ss to 3rd of 3ch.

18th-20th rounds As 17th.

21st round Ss into next ch sp, 3ch, 1tr into same sp, 2ch, *2tr into next sp, 2ch, rep from * all round. Join with a ss to 3rd of 3ch.

22nd-26th rounds As 21st.

27th round Ss into next ch sp, 3ch, 1tr into same sp, 3ch, *2tr into next sp, 3ch, rep from * all round. Join with a ss to 3rd of 3ch.

28th round Ss into next ch sp, 3ch, 1tr, 1ch, 2tr into same sp, 2ch, 2tr into next ch sp, 2ch, *2tr, 1ch, 2tr into next ch sp, 2ch, 2tr into next ch sp, 2ch, rep from * all round. Join with a ss to 3rd of 3ch. Fasten off B.
Join in C to 1ch sp.

29th round 3ch, 1tr into same sp, 2ch, 2tr into next 2ch sp, 2ch, 2tr into next 2ch sp, *2ch, 2tr into 1ch sp, 2ch, 2tr into 2ch sp, 2ch, 2tr into 2ch sp, rep from * ending with 2ch. Join with a ss to 3rd of 3ch.

30th round Ss into 2ch sp, 3ch, 1tr into same sp, 2ch, *2tr into next 2ch sp, 2ch, rep from * all round. Join with a ss to 3rd of 3ch.

31st-38th rounds As 30th.

39th round Ss into first ch sp, 3ch, 1tr into same sp, 3ch, *2tr into next ch sp, 3ch, rep from * all round. Join with a ss to 3rd of 3ch.

40th-41st rounds As 39th.

42nd round As 28th.

43rd round Ss into 1ch sp, 3ch, 1tr into same sp, 3ch, 2tr into next 2ch sp, 3ch, 2tr into next 2ch sp, *3ch, 2tr into 1ch sp, 3ch, 2tr into 2ch sp, 3ch, 2tr into 2ch sp, rep from * ending with 3ch. Join with a ss into 3rd of 3ch.

44th-45th rounds As 39th. Fasten off C.
Join in D to 3ch sp.

46th round 3ch, 1tr into same sp, 3ch, *2tr into next ch sp, 3ch, rep from * all round. Join with a ss to 3rd of 3ch.

47th-52nd rounds As 39th.

53rd round As 28th.

54th round As 43rd.

55th-65th rounds As 39th.

66th round 3ch, 1tr into next tr, 3tr into 3ch sp, *1tr into each of next 2tr, 3tr into next 3ch sp, rep from * all round. Join with a ss into 3rd of 3ch. Fasten off.

To make up
Darn in all ends. Press under a damp cloth with a warm iron.

Shaggy bear bath mat

Size

Length, 106.5cm (*42in*)
Width at widest point, 81.5cm (*32in*)

Tension

9tr and 10 rows to 10cm (*3.9in*) over patt
worked on No.3.50 (ISR) crochet hook

Materials

38 balls Twilley's Stalite in main shade, A
1 ball of contrast colour, B
One No.3.50 (ISR) crochet hook
Latchet hook
0.45 metre (½ *yard*) of 91cm (*36 inch*) wide
cotton fabric
Kapok for filling

Body section

Using No.3.50 (ISR) hook and A, make
82ch.
1st row Into 4th ch from hook work 1tr,
1tr into each ch to end. Turn. 80tr.
**2nd row 3ch to count as first tr, miss first
tr, 1tr into each tr, ending with 1tr into 3rd
of 3ch. Turn.
Rep last row 26 times more.
Shape legs
Next row 3ch, miss first tr, 2tr into next tr,
1tr into each tr to last 2 sts, 2tr into next tr,
1tr into 3rd of 3ch. Turn. 2tr increased.
Rep last row until there are 114tr.
Divide for legs
Next row 3ch, miss first tr, 1tr into each
of next 46tr, turn.
Cont on these 47tr for first leg.
Next row 3ch, miss first tr, (yrh, insert into
next tr and draw through a loop, yrh and
draw through first 2 loops on hook) twice,
yrh and draw through all loops on hook –
called dec 1tr –, 1tr into each tr to last 2 sts,
2tr into next tr, 1tr into 3rd of 3ch. Turn.
Next row 3ch, miss first tr, 2tr into next
tr, 1tr into each tr to last 3 sts, dec 1tr, 1tr
into 3rd of 3ch. Turn.
Rep last 2 rows once more.
Next row 3ch, miss first tr, dec 1tr, 1tr
into each tr, ending with 1tr into 3rd of 3ch.
Turn.
Next row Work to last 3 sts, dec 1tr, 1tr
into 3rd of 3ch. Turn.
Rep last 2 rows 4 times more. 37tr.
Next 2 rows Ss into each of first 3tr, 3ch,
work to last 2 sts, turn.
Next 2 rows Ss into each of first 4tr, 3ch,
work to last 2 sts, turn. 17tr. Fasten off.
Return to where work was divided, miss

20tr in centre, rejoin yarn to next tr, 3ch,
work to end. 47tr. Complete as given for
first leg. Reversing shaping. **. Turn work
round and rejoin yarn to first 80tr. Complete
to match other half from ** to **.

Tail

Rejoin yarn to first 20tr missed at centre
between legs.
Next row 3ch, miss first tr, dec 1tr, work to
last 3tr, dec 1tr, 1tr into last tr. Turn.
Rep last row until 2tr rem, run thread
through sts and fasten off.

Head top section

Using No.3.50 (ISR) hook and A, make 8ch.
1st row Into 4th ch from hook work 1tr,
1tr into each ch to end. Turn. 6tr.
2nd row 3ch, 1tr into first tr, 2tr into each
tr, ending with 2tr into 3rd of 3ch. Turn.
12tr.
3rd row 3ch, 1tr into first tr, 2tr into next
tr, 1tr into each tr to last 2 sts, 2tr into next
tr, 2tr into 3rd of 3ch. Turn. 4tr increased.
4th row 3ch, 1tr into first tr, 1tr into each
tr, ending with 2tr into 3rd of 3ch. Turn.
2 sts increased.
Rep 3rd and 4th rows 6 times more, then
4th row twice. 58tr.
19th row 3ch, miss first tr, 1tr into each tr,

ending with 1tr into 3rd of 3ch. Fasten off.
Turn work.
20th row Miss first 15tr, rejoin yarn to next
tr, 1tr into same place, 1tr into each of next
26tr, 2tr into next tr, turn. 30tr.
Rep (4th row, then 19th row) twice and
4th row once. Fasten off.

Head underside section

Using No.3.50 (ISR) hook and A,
make 8ch.
1st row As given for 1st row of top section.
Rep 4th row of top section 18 times, then
19th row once. Fasten off.

Ears

Using No.3.50 (ISR) hook and A, make
4ch. Join with a ss into first ch to form a
circle.
1st round Work 8dc into circle.
2nd round Work 2dc into each dc. 16dc.
3rd round As 2nd. 32dc.
4th-6th rounds Work 1dc into each dc.
7th round *1dc into next dc, 2dc into next
dc, rep from * all round. 48dc.
8th-9th rounds Work 1dc into each dc.
Fasten off.
Work another ear in A, then 2 ears in B
omitting the 9th round. Do not fasten off,
but place one ear in A and one ear in B

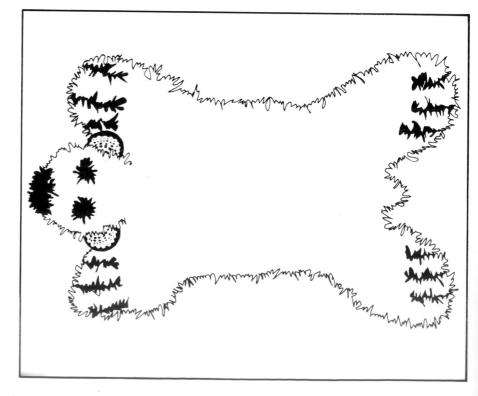

together with the ear in B in front, and work round the outer edge in dc and B, working into each st of the last round of both ears.

Complete the other ear in the same way.

To make up

Head filling Lay each piece of head section on cotton material and draw round outline, leaving 2.5cm (*1in*) free all round. Sew seams of lining, leaving an opening for stuffing. Stuff firmly with kapok and sew up opening.

Body tufting Cut A into 10cm (*4in*) lengths and using 4 strands together, beg at back feet and knot strands round each tr. Cut B in the same way and work 3 vertical rows on each paw to resemble claws.

Head Knot in the same way as for body, but work 4 rows in B for nose and patches in B for eyes. Trim any uneven threads. Beg at nose, sew top section of head to underside. Sew back seams in top section. This leaves an opening for the head filling which is removable for washing. Push filling firmly into head, moulding into shape.

Country crochet rug

Size
152.5cm × 132cm (*60in × 52in*), excluding fringe

Tension
10tr and 10 sp and 10 rows to 14cm (*5½in*) over patt worked on No.6.00 (ISR) crochet hook

Materials
15 × 50grm balls Sirdar Wash'n'Wear Chunky in main shade, A
13 balls each of contrast colours, B and C
One No.6.00 (ISR) crochet hook
Large tapestry needle or bodkin

Note
To obtain an even background, insert hook under 3 top strands of tr in previous row so working into body of st

Rug
Using No.6.00 (ISR) hook and A, make 194ch.
Base row Into 6th ch from hook work 1tr, *1ch, miss 1ch, 1tr into next ch, rep from * to end. Turn. 95 sp.
1st row 3ch to count as first tr, * 1tr into next tr, 1ch, rep from * to last sp, miss 1ch, 1tr into 4th of first 5ch. Turn.
The last row forms patt. Rep last row 3 times more. Break off A. Cont in patt

working striped sequence of 5 rows B, 5 rows C and 5 rows A throughout. Rep striped sequence 6 times more. Fasten off.

To make up
Sew in ends. Press lightly under a dry cloth with a cool iron.
Weaving Cut 70 lengths of A, 60 lengths of B and 60 lengths of C, all 223.5cm (*88in*) long. Take 2 strands of A and taking care not to twist strands, weave vertically over and under 1ch bars separating tr, beg with 1st row of sps and leaving 15cm (*6in*) hanging free. A firmer edge will be obtained if needle is passed through first ch on lower edge rather than into sp and also through final ch in top edge. Do not pull yarn too tightly, but weave at a tension that will leave 15cm (*6in*) hanging free at top edge. Work a further 4 rows in A weaving over alt bars to preceding row.
Cont in same way in striped sequence as given for rug.
Fringe Cut two 33cm (*13in*) lengths of colour required for each sp along both edges of rug. Fold strands to form a loop. Insert hook into first sp at lower edge, draw loop through, draw woven ends through loop then draw fringe ends through loop and draw up tightly. Rep along lower edge and upper edge, taking care to keep same side of rug uppermost while knotting fringe. Trim fringe.

OVERSEAS SUPPLIERS AND AGENTS

EMU
Australia: Broseley Imports, 37 Chermside Street, Highgate Hill, Brisbane 4101
Canada: S. R. Kurtzer & Co. Ltd., 275 Adelaide Street West, Toronto 129

JAEGER AND PATONS
Australia: Coats Patons (Australia) Ltd., 321/355 Fir Tree Gully Road, Mount Waverley, Victoria 3149
New Zealand: Coats Patons (N.Z.) Ltd., P.O. Box 6149, Textiles House, 48 Wyndham Street, Auckland
South Africa: Paton & Baldwin South Africa (PTY) Ltd., P.O. Box 33, Randfontein, Transvaal.
Canada: Paton & Baldwin (Canada) Ltd., 1001 Roselawn Avenue, Toronto M6B 1B8

LEE TARGET
Australia and New Zealand: M. J. Shaw & Co., 248 La Perouse Street, Redhill, A.C.T. 2603
Canada: Dutex & Co. Ltd., 1520 Antonio Barbeau, Montreal 355 TQ
South Africa: Lister Co. (S.A.) PTY Ltd., P.O. Box 1772, Cape Town

PINGOUIN
Australia and New Zealand: Panda Yarns (PTY) Ltd., Panda House, 1 Belgium Avenue, Richmond, Victoria 3121
South Africa: Ropes and Matting Holding Limited, 245 Voortreker Street, P.O. Box 12003, Jacobs 4026, Natal
Canada: International Transactions Co. Limited, 763 Boulevard Lebeau, 379 St. Laurent, Quebec

ROBIN
Australia: Broseley Imports, 37 Chermside Street, Highgate Hill, Brisbane 4101
Canada: S. R. Kurtzer & Co. Limited, 257 Adelaide Street, West, Toronto 129

SIRDAR
Australia: Sirdar Wools (Australia) PTY Ltd., P.O. Box 472, Goulborn, NSW 2580
New Zealand: Sirdar Division, Hole Proof Mills Limited, P.O. Box 2216 Auckland
South Africa: Sirdar Wools (PTY) Ltd., P.O. Box 49072, Rosettenville, Johannesburg
Canada: Diamond Yarns (Canada) Corp., 97 St. Lawrence Building, Montreal

TWILLEYS
Australia: Panda Yarns Limited, 48–56 Western Street, Brunswick 3056
New Zealand: Mosgiel Limited, Roslyn Mills, Kai Korai, Valley Road, Dunedin
South Africa: Monica Novelty Co., 139 President Street, Johannesburg
Canada: S. R. Kurtzer & Co. Limited, 257 Adelaide Street West, Toronto 129

WENDY
Australia and New Zealand: Mail Order from Carter & Parker (UK)
South Africa: Wendy Wools (PTY) Limited, P.O. Box 93, Woodstock, Capetown
Canada: Dutex & Co. Limited, 1520 Antonio Barbeau, Montreal 355 TQ

SYMBOLS

An asterisk, *, shown in a pattern row denotes that the stitches shown after this sign must be repeated from that point.
Square brackets [ ] denote instructions for larger sizes in the pattern.
Round brackets, ( ) denotes that this section of the pattern is to be worked for all sizes.
Crochet hooks have been standardized into an International Size Range, (ISR), and these sizes will be used throughout these instructions.

Terminology

UK	US
single crochet or slip stitch (ss)	slip stitch (sl st)
double crochet (dc)	single crochet (sc)
treble crochet (tr)	double crochet (dc)
half treble (htr)	half double crochet
double treble (dtr)	treble crochet (tr)
triple treble (tr tr)	double treble (dtr)
quadruple treble	triple treble (tr tr)
treble round treble	double round double
treble between	double between
treble	double

YARNS AND TENSIONS FOR OVERSEAS READERS

Yarns and qualities vary from year to year and country to country. The secret of using this book at any time, in any country, is to use a yarn which works to the right tension. To check, work up a tension sample before embarking on a garment. The hook size is only a guide—the point is to have the right number of stitches and rows to the inch. To do this you may need to use a hook size larger or smaller than suggested because some people crochet more loosely or tightly than others.
Because it is difficult to judge how to count say $3\frac{1}{2}$ or $4\frac{1}{2}$ stitches to the inch, it is worth counting stitches over four inches and then dividing by four.
If the tension reference includes a $\frac{3}{4}$, measure over three inches to get a whole number of stitches then divide by three. Even a $\frac{1}{4}$ of a stitch in an inch should be considered if a 36in sweater in double knitting yarn has a $\frac{1}{4}$ stitch to the inch too few, the finished garment will be almost 2 inches too tight. Some yarns made overseas carry the same name as a similar British yarn but are made up to a different specification always double check with a tension square. In some cases, yarns work up to the same number of stitches to the inch but give a slightly different number of rows to the inch, but an experienced crochet worker should be able to adjust garment lengths to her own requirements.
When you use a yarn different from the one originally quoted, you may need a different number of balls or ounces, so keep a spare ball showing the dye lot number.